WORLD OF EMBELLISHMENT

ADD GLOBAL DESIGNS TO CONTEMPORARY FASHIONS & DÉCOR

JOAN HINDS

Published by

700 East State Street • Iola, WI 54990-0001
715/445-2214 • FAX: 715/445-4087   www.krause.com

Krause Publications
700 E. State St., Iola, WI 54990-0001

Please call or write for our free catalog of publications. Our toll-free number to place an order or obtain a free catalog is 800-258-0929, or please use our regular business telephone 715-445-2214.

Photography by Jeff Frey & Associates.
Illustrations by Kathy Marsaa.
Project designs by Joan Hinds, unless otherwise noted.

Library of Congress Catalog Number: 2002107602

ISBN: 0-87349-434-2

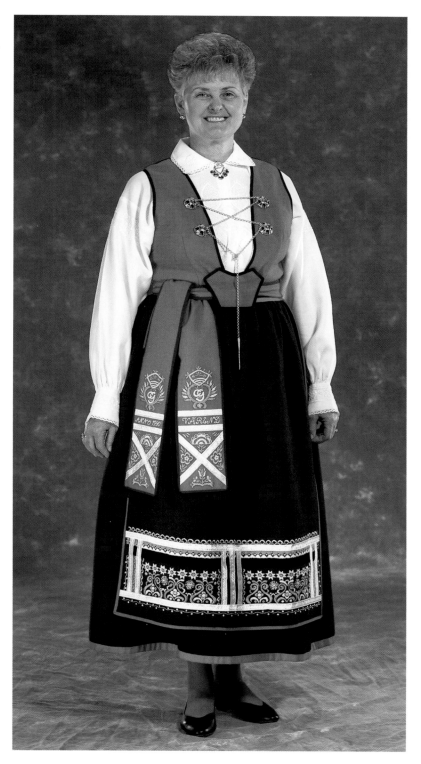

Dedication

World of Embellishment is dedicated to all the folk artists of the past and present. May they continue to pass on their culture to future generations through textile techniques, designs, and embroidery.

Acknowledgments

I could not have completed this book without the help and support of many people. My sincere thanks and appreciation go to:

Marilee Sagat, Karen Cermak, and Marlene Gaige from the Twin Cities, and Duluthian Char Harkins, for their friendship and enthusiastic design assistance. Marilee, Karen, and Char receive my undying gratitude for their fabulous project contributions to this book.

George Lokken, Jill Lakhan, Cathy Nelson, Shanti Lakhan, Erna Peterson, Alphea Iverson, Bobby Gaige, Rolf Hagberg, Rachael Martin of Glensheen, and Jan Ringer, for the loan of materials, treasured family heirlooms, and historical textiles from other lands.

My illustrator, Kathy Marsaa, for her wonderful drawings to complement my instructions; and Tigg and Rolf from Jeff Frey Photography for the incredible creativity used to highlight my creations. A picture is indeed worth a thousand words.

Models, Sue Anderson, Mary Beth Tarnowski, Stina Lapaugh, Char Harkins, Shanti Lakhan, Erna Peterson, Alphea Iverson, and Rebecca Hinds, for the gracious donations of their time.

My husband, Fletcher, who was willing to help make a design decision no matter what time of the night, my son, Kevin, for his computer literacy, and my daughter, Rebecca, for her flair for color and design.

The staff at Krause Publications for allowing me to share my passion with the other sewing enthusiasts. A special thank you goes to Julie Stephani for her encouragement, and to my editor, Jodi Rintelman, for her patience and guidance.

Back of George Lokken's Ojibwa vest.

Table of Contents

Glossary

AWAY KNOT—A knot made in the thread used for needlework. The knot lies on the right side of the fabric several inches from the beginning of the stitching. After the stitching is completed, the knot is cut off and the thread is woven into the stitching on the back to secure.

BASTE—A long running stitch to hold fabrics or trim in place temporarily before they are sewn together.

COUCH—A thread or trim that is too thick to pass through fabric is laid on the surface and a small stitch is taken over the thread or trim to hold it in place.

FLOAT—A thread is carried over the top of a trim before it is stitched again.

GUSSET—An extra piece of fabric sewn into a garment or accessory that allows extra room.

PLACKET—The opening in a garment that facilitates putting it on and taking it off.

STITCH IN THE DITCH—Actually sewing on the seam line of two fabrics. The stitching will not be seen on the right side.

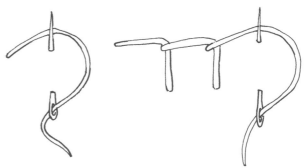

BLANKET STITCH and BUTTON-HOLE STITCH—These terms are ofen used interchangeably. The stitch was traditionally used to finish the edges of blankets. When stitched close together, it will form a row of knots along a cut edge. This stitch is also used for buttonholes or cutwork embroidery. Today's sewing machines often have it built in for appliqué or decorative stitching.

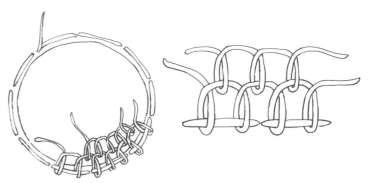

A detached blanket/buttonhole stitch is loosely worked on a foundation of straight stitches. The blanket/buttonhole stitch loops over the straight stitch and does not pierce the fabric. Each consecutive row of stitches is worked in the loops of the previous row.

Rebecca Hinds models the Scandinavian Jacket.

Introduction

Folk art and folk costume have always been interests of mine, but I recently began studying clothing and textile embellishment as it pertained to doll costuming. As I perused folk art and textile books and viewed examples in museums, I learned more about the everyday life of other cultures. The working class populations decorated utilitarian objects and clothing with traditional designs. The reasons for the use of certain motifs, styles, and materials were based on necessity and the environmental conditions of each culture. Women (as well as men) created beautiful and practical clothing and textiles that kept them warm, cool, dry, and safe from evil. The folk art prominently displayed on clothing and household textiles was passed down from generation to generation.

Our American society is adapting to the influence of many more cultures than ever before. As we adopt foods, art, and clothing in our everyday life, we can become more tolerant of others. As we "blend" together as a society, many cultural clothing styles and designs will also become "blended." It has become clear to me that folk art history, designs, and costume from some cultures will soon be lost in our rapidly evolving multicultural society.

My intent in writing this book is to celebrate the colors, embroidery, clothing styles, and designs seen in folk costume and textiles from various cultures around the world. By incorporating small bits of embellishment or clothing silhouettes into today's fashion and décor, we will continue to honor and preserve our own cultural heritage and discover folk art from other less familiar cultures.

This sheepskin vest from Slovakia has intricately patterned red leather appliqués stitched on the front and back. The inside of the vest still has the wool attached to the skin for warmth. (From the collection of Cathy Nelson.)

How Costume Styles Developed

From the beginning of time, humans have needed to cover their bodies and to create functional household items. The clothing and textiles that developed were decorated using indigenous materials and traditional designs.

Many factors have influenced the clothing silhouettes, such as climate and required body movement. The most important of these factors has been the availability of materials and tools used to create the variety of styles seen around the world and throughout history. For example, if animal skins were used, as in North America, the clothing was designed with the animal size and shape as the defining factor. The techniques for sewing the skins together and the embellishment with beads, teeth, quills, etc. developed over time.

Other societies developed woven cloth, and the loom size determined the width of the cloth. If looms were small, garments tended to be narrow and tight as in Eastern Asia. If they were large, as in Greek and Roman times, draping was a common clothing style.

As civilization developed, other factors influenced costume styles and embellishment. Communities were self-sufficient so that influence from outside cultures was minimal. Social identity was noted through clothing and its embellishment. Colors and patterns were distinctive of the wearer's area or tribe. Some will say that there was little choice in the traditional costumes in a society, but a walk through a suburban mall today would reveal that the modern wardrobe does not hold much more variety. Very similar jeans, t-shirts, and athletic shoes are found in many stores.

The folk art and costume in a community developed from everyday activities, such as farming and food preparation. In Eastern Europe, the shafts of wheat tied into crowns for young women represented the harvest. Special clothing evolved for celebrations, weddings, feast days, and carnivals. Elaborate decoration for this ceremonial clothing could be seen as a display of wealth.

Many cultures and ethnic groups have crossed physical boundaries and borders throughout history. Costumes and textile embellishment were influenced by conquering empires throughout history. North Africa has a large rectangular draped costume called a *haik* that was based on the Roman toga. Styles and designs in Europe and Asia show the widespread influence of the Ottoman Empire. The Americas have indigenous styles, but they have been greatly altered by the influence of European materials and designs. Thus, it has been difficult to credit a clothing style or design motif to one particular country. It is easier to describe regions of the world that have similar climates, lifestyles, and folk art.

In spite of the different materials and styles of textiles and dress throughout the world, many similarities can be noted in the embellishment of such articles. The most common method of embellishment has been done for centuries with a needle and thread. The thread may be as varied as moose hair, silk, or long thin strands of metal, but many similar stitches developed all over the globe. Knotted, looped, and flat stitches are the basis of all embroidery. The running stitch and its variations, such as the darning stitch, are prevalent in many cultures. The satin stitch, a type of flat stitch, is seen in Europe, the Middle East, Asia, India, and North Africa. Cross stitch and chain stitch embroidery are widely used throughout the world.

Embellishments for textiles and clothing have more variation, due to the accessibility of materials. Beads, mirrors, quills, coins, sequins, tassels, fringes, feathers, and shells have been used for decoration. Shiny items that reflect light are seen to protect the wearer from the evil eye, and may represent water that may be scarce in desert localities. Precious metals have been used on clothing for persons of rank, such as the clergy or the military. Beads and other materials have been used for trade between cultures. But above all, people want to feel beautiful by adorning themselves with decorative clothing.

Embroidered cuffs from blouse sleeves are often cut off and saved for future use. Both the cuffs feature "wolves' teeth," narrow strips of cloth that are folded to resemble sharp points on each side. The use of wolves' teeth on clothing ensures the wearer protection from evil. (From the collection of Cathy Nelson.)

This ruffled lace collar and sleeve with gold embroidery are part of a blouse from Slovakia. (From the collection of Cathy Nelson.)

Create Your Own World of Embellishment

Incorporating embellishments from other cultures can be easier than you think. Since many clothing styles and decorative techniques overlap, I have divided the projects by regions around the world instead of by individual countries. Vests are prevalent throughout all of Europe, but I have only featured one from Eastern Europe. You may want to make a vest and decorate it with the wool embroidery from the German Sweater-Jacket. You may prefer to put the Shisha embroidery on a tunic or jacket rather than a placemat. This book will give you the tools to embellish many different fashions and décor with global designs.

Our clothing and textile items today have a much more tailored look than some other cultures, particularly in Europe. Traditional dirndl skirts from Austria and Bavaria are lovely and may show an individual's wealth, since a large amount of fabric is required. Not everyone today wants to wear such a full skirt. A way to adapt clothing styles from this area is to focus on men's wear. Men wore beautifully embellished and trimmed jackets and pants that can be incorporated into a contemporary wardrobe. Look to both men's and women's costume from around the world for more inspiration.

Ready-made garments and accessories can easily be decorated with folk art designs from other cultures. You will not have to construct everything from scratch. Purchased jackets and blazers are perfect backdrops for embellishment or embroidery. Look for plain or tweed fabrics. Purchased table linens are often made with plain fabrics that lend themselves to decoration. Time can be saved on basic construction while you devote more effort to the embellishment.

The materials used in most clothing and textiles are natural fibers, such as silk, cotton, or linen. This is understandable since the styles have been developed over centuries and synthetics are relatively new. It may be difficult to locate these fibers in threads and fabrics in some areas. Try using blends, such as a linen-cotton blend or a silk-rayon blend. The effect will probably be very similar to the original.

Modern methods and tools of sewing and needlework can be used to create techniques of the past. All embroidery was originally done by hand. Now we have embroidery capabilities in some sewing machines. These machines can stitch embroidered motifs that have an ethnic flavor to them. Braids and trims have been couched by hand but now can be sewn with zigzag stitches and a clear invisible thread. Don't be afraid to use adhesives to help secure your fabrics and trims for sewing. A water-soluble glue stick is a must to hold tiny trims to fabric before stitching. Temporary adhesive sprays can hold appliqués in place before sewing.

Marking design lines on dark opaque fabrics or ready-made items can be difficult because the design cannot be seen through the fabric for tracing. Drawing on fabrics that have a nap such as velveteen may be more difficult. I like to trace the design on a tissue paper pattern with a pencil or marker. Pin the tissue paper pattern on the garment, accessory, or fabric area to be embellished. With a needle and contrasting thread, baste the pattern to the fabric with approximately ¼" stitches. When the design is completely basted, tear the paper off the fabric. Now you can stitch over the basting, easily pulling out any threads that may show on the surface.

The supply lists for the projects may not always have exact amounts. If the project involves ready-made clothing or purchased textiles, I have given only approximate amounts for the trims, since size will determine the exact measurements. If the project is made from scratch, all the amounts for the materials will be listed.

I urge you to explore the world of embellishment and create your own fashions and décor with an ethnic flair!

An assortment of embroidered pieces from China. The child's boots have dragon motifs with thread fringe for the beard.

The people of North America used original materials for clothing and embellishment that were derived from their surroundings. They used fur and animal skins, plant fibers like yucca or cedar bark, cotton, porcupine quills, and shells. Each area had access to different types of raw materials, so there were big differences in clothing and decoration within nations.

The Plains Indian style of dress is probably the most familiar. The basic dress or robe has a yoke or straps and is made from animal skins. Decorations include beadwork, feathers, and embroidery. The Northwest Coast Indians used woven cedar bark for blankets and waterproof robes. These were decorated with motifs using an "eye" form placed inside squared-off oval shapes. In the southwest, women wore aprons made of strips of yucca or other plants.

With the European influence, clothing and textiles underwent a dramatic change. The introduction of the horse precipitated a change from a long robe or shirt to shorter tunics and leggings. Small glass beads from Europe replaced the shell beads that were used for *wampum*. Most of the quillwork was replaced by beadwork. In the southwest, Spanish settlers introduced sheep, and the art of wool blanket weaving began. The stylized designs of the Europeans, such as flowers and birds, were integrated into Native American decoration.

This vest with traditional Ojibwa beadwork was made for George Lokken on the Red Lake Reservation.

Northwest Coast Indian Button Blanket Pillow

Supplies:

- ⅓ yd. red broadcloth
- 1 yd. blue broadcloth
- Scraps of yellow and blue-green broadcloth
- Fusible web
- 14" pillow form
- 1¾ yd. cording, ¼" diameter
- 1 skein white embroidery floss
- 56 white buttons, ⅛"
- 30 white buttons, ⅜"
- 11 white buttons, ¼"

The Tlingit people of the Northwest coast had the famous *Chilkat* blanket as part of their ceremonial costume. It was woven with a warp of cedar bark twisted with goat hair and a weft of only goat hair. The patterns consisted of stylized animals, birds, and fish with human-like faces. The Hudson's Bay Company brought with them blankets and mother-of-pearl buttons. These were incorporated into the Tlingit culture. The ceremonial "Button Blanket" appeared in the middle of the nineteenth century. A heavy dark blue material, such as a Hudson's Bay blanket, had a center appliqué of red flannel that depicted a crest figure, usually an animal, fish, or bird. The red border and the crest were outlined with rows of mother-of-pearl buttons. Today the crest figures are no longer the property of a family and are designed as the maker prefers.

I have chosen to make a "Button Blanket" pillow, using the traditional colors of the Tlingits. The fabric, however, is cotton broadcloth, not wool flannel. Wide red fabric strips border the blue center. The appliquéd design in the center is a turtle, surrounded by rows of white buttons. (The buttons around the turtle's head are mother-of-pearl buttons from my grandmother's stash.) I chose a turtle as my "crest figure," because I like to follow the motto "slow and steady wins the race."

All seam allowances for this project are ½".

1 Cut a 10" square of blue broadcloth for the front and a 15" square of blue broadcloth for the back. Cut four strips of red broadcloth, 3½" x 15", for the front.

2 With right sides together, sew one of the strips to one side of the blue front, centering the strip on the square so that 2½" extends from each end. Sew another strip to another side of the front as before, mitering the corners. Press open. Repeat with all the strips. Press seam allowances around the square toward the red fabric strips.

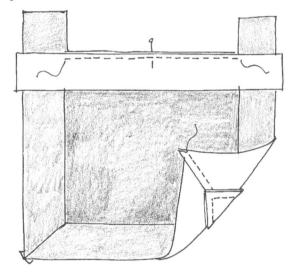

3 Trace the turtle, outer shell, and inner shell pattern pieces on the paper side of the fusible web. Peel the paper off the other side and stick the turtle on red broadcloth, each of the outer shell pattern pieces on the blue-green broadcloth, and the inner shell pieces on yellow broadcloth. Cut one turtle. Cut one each of the outer shell pieces and one each of the inner shell pieces.

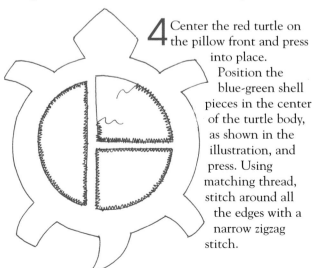

4 Center the red turtle on the pillow front and press into place. Position the blue-green shell pieces in the center of the turtle body, as shown in the illustration, and press. Using matching thread, stitch around all the edges with a narrow zigzag stitch.

5 Position the yellow inner shell pieces on the blue-green shell pieces, as shown in the illustration. Using matching thread, stitch around each piece with a narrow zigzag stitch.

6 Sew the buttons around the outside of the turtle. All of the ¼" buttons are stitched around the head of the turtle. All but seven of the ⅛" buttons are stitched to the feet and tail of the turtle. The ⅜" buttons are stitched around the body of the turtle. The seven remaining buttons are stitched to the center of the yellow shell pieces, according to the markings on the pattern pieces.

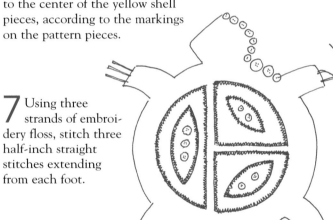

7 Using three strands of embroidery floss, stitch three half-inch straight stitches extending from each foot.

8 Cut 1⅔ yards of 1½" wide blue bias for piping. Fold the bias over the cording and sew close to the cord using a piping foot or zipper foot on the sewing machine. Trim the seam allowance of the piping to ½" if necessary.

9 Sew piping to the outside edges of the pillow front, overlapping the ends in the seam allowance.

10 With right sides together, sew the pillow back to the front. Leave approximately 10" of one of the sides open. Stuff the pillow through the opening. Fold the seam allowance of the pillow back to the inside, and slipstich the opening closed.

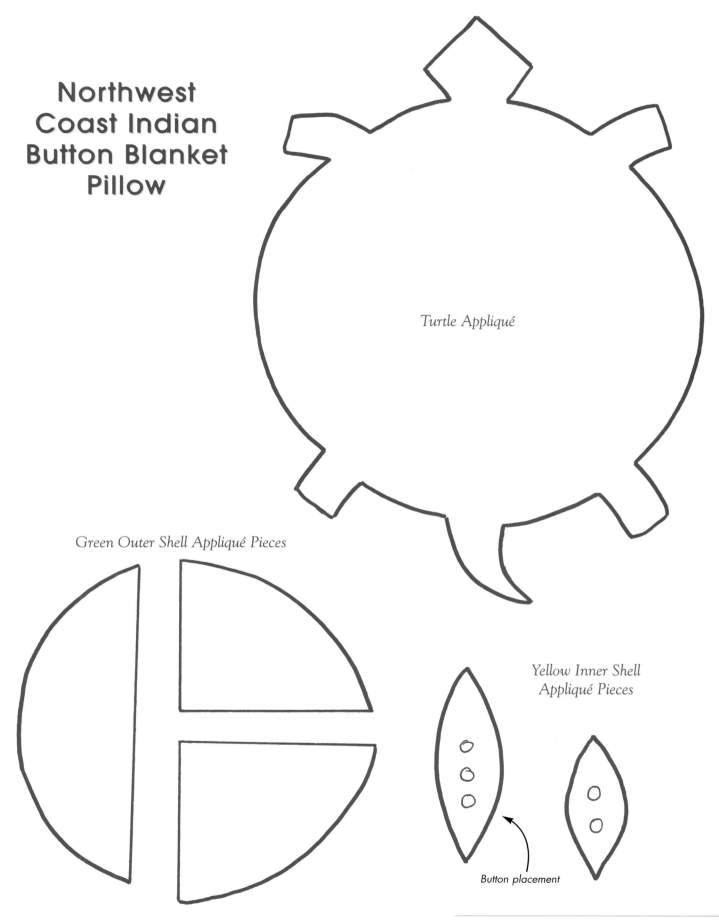

Northwest Coast Indian Button Blanket Pillow

Turtle Appliqué

Green Outer Shell Appliqué Pieces

Yellow Inner Shell Appliqué Pieces

Button placement

Ojibwa Beaded Box

Supplies:

- Black oval fabric box with removable lid, 5½" long
- 8" square of black velveteen
- Size 11 opaque beads, 1 hank each in light and medium green, coral, and red
- Size 11 yellow opaque beads, approximately 15
- Size 11 blue opaque beads, approximately 140
- #10 tapestry beading needles
- Nymo beading thread
- Chalk marker
- Lightweight plastic or cardboard
- Fabric glue, such as Fabri-tac®

(Designed by Karen Cermak)

The Ojibwa lived in Michigan, Wisconsin, and Minnesota near the upper Great Lakes. Before the Europeans arrived, the Ojibwa were doing beadwork with wood, porcupine quills, stones, copper, and shells. Needles were made from animal bones, and thread was from deer sinew. In the early seventeenth century, Europeans introduced glass beads. Beads were a valuable and commonly traded item during the Fur Trade era. The price for one hank of beads was equal to one muskrat skin. The Ojibwa word for bead is *manidoominens*, which means "tiny spirit berry."

The Ojibwa lived in the woodlands, so the designs for their beadwork were botanical. Patterns were designed with symmetry, since balance and harmony were highly valued. An unbalanced design would show disrespect to the spirits of the world from which the designs were taken.

Beadwork was often stitched on black velveteen fabric, as was done with this project. This black satin box has a removable lid. The glass beads, which should be opaque, are stitched to the black velvet. After the stitching, the fabric is cut to fit over the cover and glued in place.

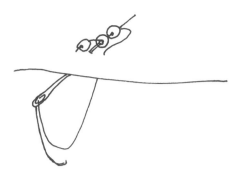

Come back up between the first and second beads, and go through beads two and three again. Pick up three more beads, and repeat the procedure until the stem motif is filled in. (This is called the beaded backstitch.)

3 Work each motif from the outside of the design to the center, switching colors as shown in the photo. When you reach the center, you may not be able to follow in rows, so put five to six beads on the needle and couch down individually with another needle and Nymo thread.

1 Use a chalk marker to trace the shape of the box insert on the velveteen. Make a template of the floral motif out of lightweight plastic or cardboard. Center the template on velveteen, and use the chalk marker to trace around it.

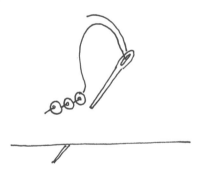

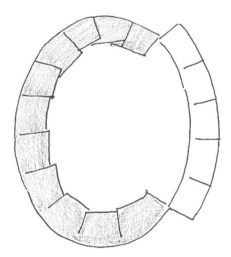

2 Thread one of the needles with a long length of thread, and knot. Come from the back of the fabric at the edge of the stem. Put three medium green beads on the needle and go back through the fabric very close to the bead on the design line.

4 When the design is completed, cut out the box insert oval approximately 1" from the traced line. Press the fabric only from the wrong side if necessary. Place the oval on the back of the design. Bring the edges of the fabric over the oval and glue with fabric glue.

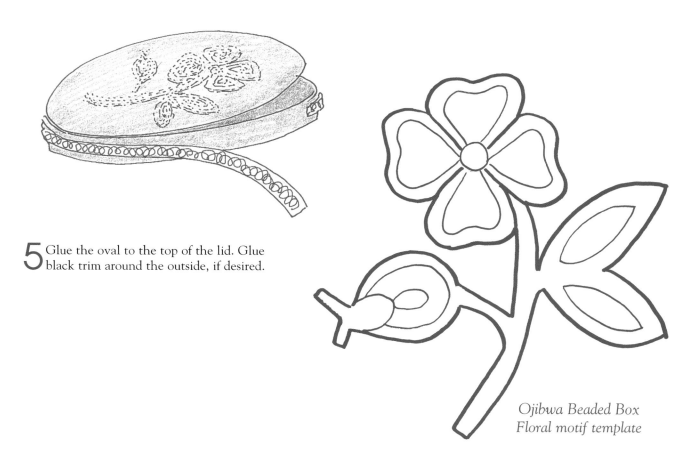

5 Glue the oval to the top of the lid. Glue black trim around the outside, if desired.

*Ojibwa Beaded Box
Floral motif template*

Close-up of bead design.

Mexico and Central America

Most of us identify the bright colors of the rainbow with the folk art of Mexico and Central America. Both the woven and embroidered fabrics of these areas feature bright reds, pinks, and blues due to the availability of natural dyes. The influence of colonization has been great, but some Indians are maintaining pre-Columbian dress by using the indigenous narrow backstrap loom. One of the garments for women is the *huipil*. It is a long blouse made of three loom-widths of fabric. It is folded in half with a hole cut for the head and the sides are stitched under the arms. The neck edge has a square neckline, which is richly embroidered, showing floral motifs from both Indian and Spanish influence. It is worn with a wrap skirt, sash, and shawl. Weavings have a variety of bird and plant motifs. Corn is considered a sacred gift from the gods and is often stylized in woven fabric.

A Mola from Panama.

Mexican Floral Frame

Supplies:

- Flat wood frame with a 5" x 7" opening, outside dimensions are 8" x 10"
- ½ yd. yellow cotton fabric
- 1⅛ yd. multi-colored braided trim, ⅝"
- 1 yd. multi-colored braided trim, ⅜"
- Purple, pink, and orange felt for appliqués
- Machine embroidery thread, orange, yellow, lavender, purple, light and dark green
- 10" x 12" thin batting
- Tear-away stabilizer
- Staple gun with staples
- Fast drying fabric glue such as Fabri-tac
- Brown paper or fabric, such as Ultrasuede®, for backing

(By Joan Hinds and Char Harkins)

The *huipil*, a traditional woven blouse with a square neckline, is often embroidered with brightly colored flowers and leaves. The same shaped flower is repeated around the neckline, alternating the colors. The centers of the flowers tend to be yellow. When the neckline is laid flat, it forms a square frame of floral embroidery.

Looking at these frames of flowers, I envisioned using this theme for an actual decorative picture frame. The frame is covered with batting and fabric that is wrapped around to the backside and stapled. Flowers and leaves are stitched to felt using a program formatted for embroidery sewing machines. The felt gives the open unstitched areas of the petals different colored backgrounds and will not ravel when cut. The flowers and leaves are arranged on the frame with each side mirroring the opposite side and glued into place.

If you have machine embroidery capabilities:

1 Choose an embroidery design formatted for your machine that has a variety of flowers and leaves. The flowers I chose ranged in size from ⅞" to 1¼" and have open spaces in the petals so that the felt colors show through.

2 Using machine embroidery thread, stitch flower appliqués on felt with stabilizer underneath. Stitch six large flowers, 10 medium flowers, and eight small flowers in your choice of colors. The flowers all have yellow centers.

3 Stitch four three-leaf clusters and four small leaves from the dark green thread. Stitch 12 medium leaves with the light green thread.

4 Tear off the stabilizer and cut close to the stitching.

If you do not have access to machine embroidery:

Cut out flower shapes from felt in a variety of colors and sizes as described above. Cut out small circles of felt for the centers. Cut out leaves from two shades of green felt.

Frame:

1 Trace the inner and outer outline of the frame onto batting and cut out. Glue the batting to the top of the frame.

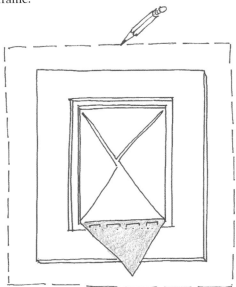

2 Place the frame face down on the wrong side of the fabric. Trace an outline 2" beyond the outer edge and cut out. Trace a line along the inner edge. Make a slit in the center of the inner square and slash to within ¼" of each corner. Fold the fabric of one of the inner sides to the back of the frame. Pull tightly and staple to the inner edge, just inside the lip of the frame.

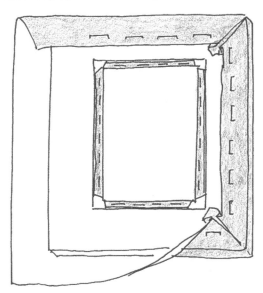

3 Repeat the process along the outer edge and staple to the back of the frame. Continue pulling and stapling each inner and outer side of the frame. Cut off any excess fabric close to the staples. Make small pleats in the corners, pull to the back of the frame, and staple.

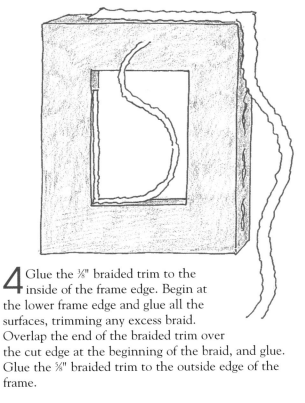

4 Glue the ⅜" braided trim to the inside of the frame edge. Begin at the lower frame edge and glue all the surfaces, trimming any excess braid. Overlap the end of the braided trim over the cut edge at the beginning of the braid, and glue. Glue the ⅜" braided trim to the outside edge of the frame.

5 Arrange the flowers and leaves, as shown in the photo, and glue in place.

6 Put a favorite photo or a mirror in the frame, and secure with staples. Cut a piece of brown paper or Ultrasuede to fit the backside, and glue along the outer edges.

Guatemalan Table Runner

Supplies:

- 1½ yd. turquoise linen/cotton blend fabric
- ½ yd. striped fabric
- 15" x 7" fuchsia cotton fabric
- 10" x 5" orange cotton fabric
- 3" x 3" yellow cotton fabric
- Fuchsia, orange, and yellow machine embroidery threads
- Tear-away stabilizer
- 1½ yd. fusible interfacing
- Clear invisible thread
- Fusible web

The Guatemalans weave all their fabric on a pre-Columbian back-strap loom. This loom produces narrow strips of cloth that are then sewn together. The woven fabric often has a multi-colored stripe pattern. Warm colors represent excitement and passion. Blue represents the sky and the spirit, while green stands for transitions in life.

Festive occasions call for brightly colored table décor. This natural fiber table runner is decorated with small patches of striped fabric from Guatemala, but any striped fabric will work. Four patches are sewn together to create a square with a "pinwheel" pattern formed with the stripes. These are stitched to the runner with clear invisible thread. Pink, orange, and yellow flowers are appliquéd in between the striped squares. The edges of the runner are stitched with machine embroidery thread and a row of decorative built-in cross-stitches. Braid or other trim can be used in place of the stitching, if desired.

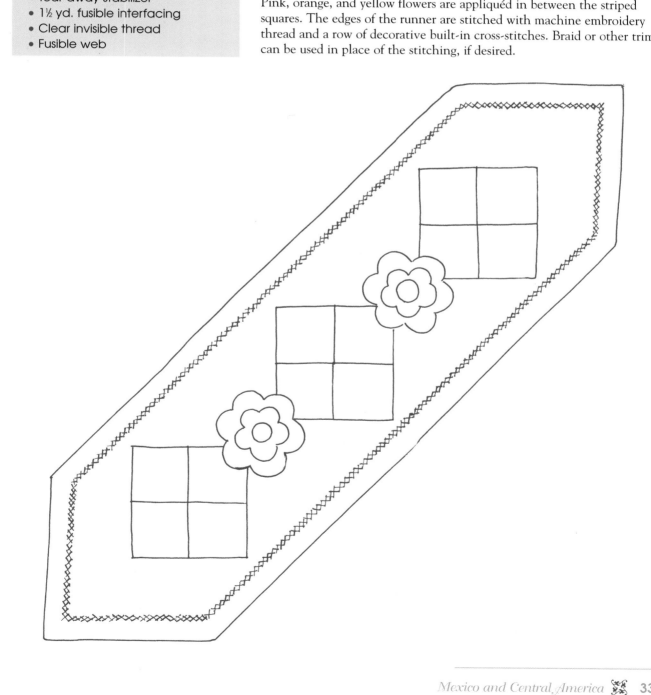

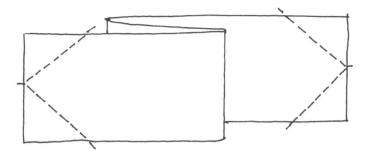

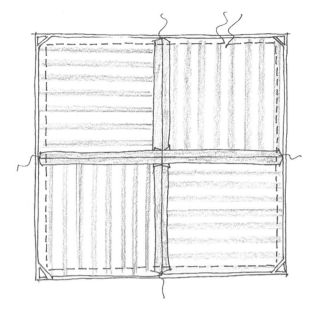

1 Cut two 50" x 15" turquoise rectangles for the table runner and its lining. Find the center of one of the 15" sides of the table runner. Measure 7½" along the top and bottom of the 50" sides of the runner. Draw a diagonal line from the center mark to the 7½" marks on the top and bottom. Cut along these lines to create a point at the end of the runner. Repeat with the other side and the lining.

2 Cut the interfacing to fit the lining of the table runner, saving the scraps of the interfacing. Fuse to the wrong side of the lining. Set aside.

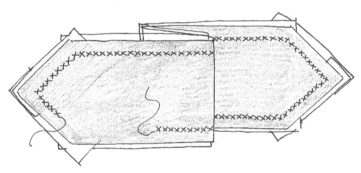

3 Cut narrow strips of stabilizer to fit under all the edges of the runner. Using the fuchsia embroidery thread, stitch a decorative stitch, such as a cross-stitch, 1½" from all edges. (If you do not have built-in decorative stitches, work a cross-stitch by hand with embroidery floss.) Tear off the stabilizer.

4 Cut twelve 4½" squares of striped fabric. Each square should have an identical pattern. With ½" seam allowances, stitch four of the squares together. The stripe pattern should alternate so that a pinwheel pattern is created. Cut a piece of interfacing to fit each square. With the wrong side of the interfacing placed on the right side of each square, stitch around the square with ½" seam allowances. Clip the corners and trim the seam allowances. Slash the back of the interfacing and turn right side out. The fusible side of the interfacing is now on the outside of the back of the squares.

5 Place the striped squares on the runner, creating a diamond pattern. The first one is 7¾" from the point of the runner and 2½" from each side of the runner. The second is placed 2¼" from the first, and the third is 2¼" from the second. Press to fuse into place. Using clear invisible thread, zigzag stitch the squares to the runner.

6 From the pattern pieces, draw two of the large flowers, two of the medium flowers, and two flower centers on the paper side of the fusible web. Place the fuchsia fabric on the fusible side of the web, and cut out the large flowers. Place the orange fabric on the fusible side of the web, and cut out the medium flowers. Place the yellow fabric on the fabric side of the web, and cut out the two centers. Peel off the papers. Place the medium flower on the center of the large flower. Place a yellow center in the middle of the medium flower. Press into place between two of the squares. Repeat with the other appliqué pieces.

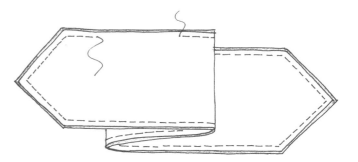

7 Using matching thread and stabilizer underneath, satin stitch around each section of the flowers. Tear away the stabilizer.

8 Pin the table runner and the lining right sides together. Stitch around the edges with ½" seam allowances, leaving an opening on one side. Trim the corners, turn to the right side, and press. Slipstitch the opening closed.

Close-up of appliqué.

Guatemalan Table Runner

Large Flower

Flower Center

Medium Flower

Guatemalan Placemat

Supplies:

- 14½" x 20" striped fabric for each placemat (stripe goes widthwise)
- 2½" x 4" striped fabric for top of pocket (stripe goes lengthwise)
- 8" x 4" turquoise linen for pocket
- 32 wooden beads (½") in three different colors
- Clear invisible thread

The placemat was designed to complement the Guatemalan Table Runner. The fabric for the placemat is the same as the striped square motifs on the runner. The side edges of the placemat are fringed with beads tied on. (If you plan to machine wash the placemat, the beads should be removed first.) A pocket for silverware is constructed from the linen fabric of the runner and has fringed striped fabric at the top. A leftover embroidered flower from the Mexican Floral Frame made a perfect decoration for the pocket!

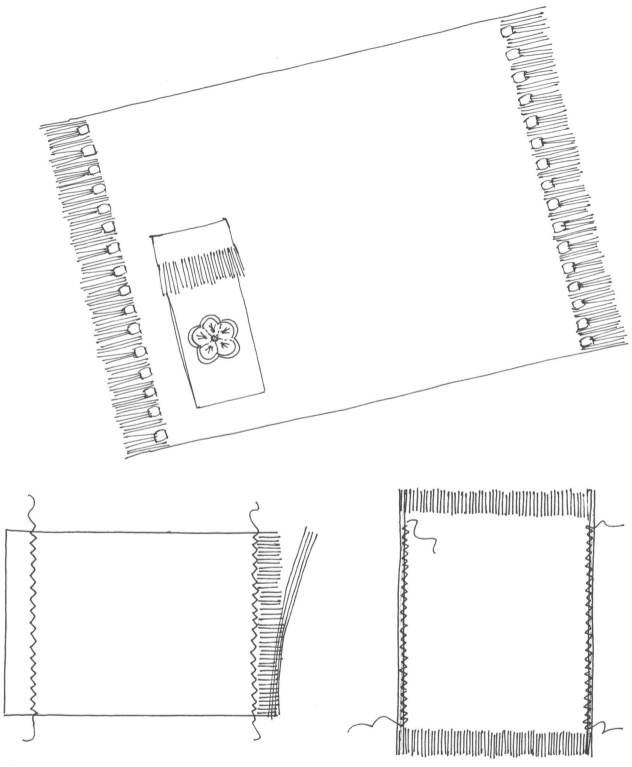

1 Measure 2" from each 14½" edge of the striped fabric, and draw a line with washout marker or chalk. Using clear invisible thread, zigzag stitch along these lines. Pull out the lengthwise threads beyond the stitching to create a 2" long fringe on each side.

2 Press the two remaining edges ¼" to the wrong side and zigzag stitch.

3 Measure 1" from one side of the 4" edge of the remaining striped fabric piece, and draw a line as in Step #2. Zigzag stitch along this line with clear invisible thread. Pull out the crosswise threads beyond the stitching to create a 1" long fringe.

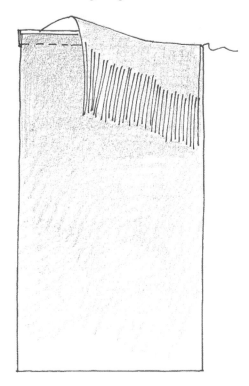

4 Pin the right side of the 4" unfringed fabric edge to the wrong side of one of the 4" sides of the turquoise linen. Stitch with a ½" seam allowance. Fold the fringed fabric to the right side of the linen, and press.

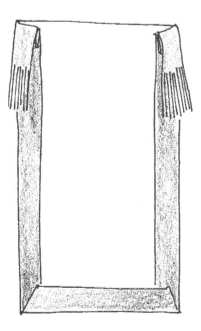

5 Press the three remaining edges of the linen ½" to the wrong side, including the striped fabric.

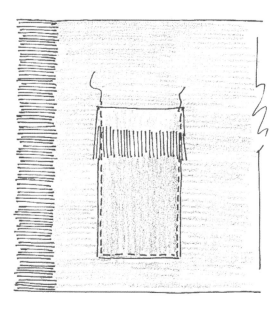

6 Place the linen pocket on the placemat so that the bottom of the pocket is 1½" from the bottom of the placemat and 1" from the side of the placemat (not including the fringe). Stitch around the three sides close to the folded edges. An extra flower appliqué from the Mexican Floral Frame (page 28) can be attached to the pocket, if desired. Use a fusible web under the appliqué, and iron it in place.

7 A few threads from the edge of the fringe, take a section of fringed threads that will fit into a bead. Pull threads all the way into the bead and divide them into two sections. Tie a knot with the two sections to hold the beads on the fringe. Evenly space 16 beads on each side of the placemat.

Scandinavians maintain the traditions of their clothing and folk art in contemporary culture. *Hardanger*, a well-known form of counted thread embroidery, and *rosmaling,* a type of decorative floral painting, are actively practiced in Scandinavia and North America. Women's clothing consists of a blouse, sleeveless vest or bodice, skirt, and apron, similar in silhouette to clothing elsewhere in Western Europe. Silver jewelry with small shallow concave disks dangling from a larger disc is worn as brooches and earrings. The dangling discs reflect the firelight, which is helpful in areas with limited sunlight. Men wear decorated jackets and breeches.

North of the Arctic Circle is home to the nomadic reindeer-herding *Samis*, often called Laplanders. This unique ethnic group crosses national borders above the Arctic Circle in Northern Norway, Sweden, Finland, and Russia. The traditional costume consists of royal blue and red tunics and skirts decorated by brightly colored braids and ribbons. Yellow is commonly used on shoulder inserts. Trousers are worn under the tunics with reindeer hide boots. The boots have an upward curve at the tip, which helps get skis on and off. Caps of many varieties are worn, such as the "cap of four winds." It has a wide headband and a crown of four corners decorated with streamers. It acquired its name from the fact that they live so close to the North Pole where the winds can come from all four directions at once. Variations of these and other caps are seen at ski hills today.

Alphea Iverson models her black wool bunad from Hallingdal, Norway. The floral motifs on the unique cap, narrow bodice, and hem are embroidered with strands of colorful wool. Note the beautiful silver jewelry.

Rebecca Hinds models the Scandinavian Jacket and Scandinavian Purse.

Scandinavian Jacket

Supplies:

- Pattern for hip length outerwear jacket that has a stand-up collar and dropped shoulders*
- Black medium weight wool fabric
- 4" x 4" square each of red, gold, and green wool felt
- Cotton print lining
- Green Lycra® strips (2½" wide) for binding
- Double-stick fusible web
- Clear invisible thread
- Light green and gold machine embroidery thread
- 6 braided trims (for size 12, I used):

  2 yd. of one ⅜" braid   2½ yd. of another ⅜" braid
  2⅛ yd. of ⅝" braid   1⅓ yd. of one ⅞" braid
  3½ yd. of another ⅞" braid   1 yd. of 1" braid

- Medium rickrack in green, red, and yellow
- Red satin cord
- 3 pewter fasteners (each side is 1¾" long)

*I used Butterick #3306.

I have designed an outerwear wool jacket based on the *Sami* tunic. It is trimmed with Scandinavian woven braids, rickrack, and satin cord. The dropped shoulders allow for braid placement and the front overlaps for a side opening fastened with Scandinavian pewter clasps. The front is also decorated with a Swedish folk art appliqué. Made from wool felt, it is easy to sew since no raw edges need to be covered. Another fast technique is the Lycra® binding around the sleeves, hem, and front edges. A woven fabric works best on this jacket, since stretching may occur while stitching the braid in place. If desired, you can back a knit fabric with stabilizer or another woven fabric before sewing the braids.

1 Before cutting the jacket and lining, extend the center of each front jacket pattern piece (4½" for size 12). This will make an overlap for a side-opening jacket. Remove the seam allowances on the top edge only of the collar, as this edge will be bound with Lycra® strip. Remove the hem of the jacket front, jacket back, and sleeves. These edges will be bound also. Cut out two jacket fronts, one jacket back, one collar, and two sleeves from the black medium weight wool fabric. (There will be no facings.) Repeat with cotton print lining.

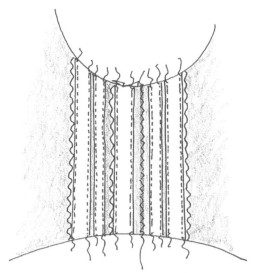

2 Sew shoulder seams with right sides together. Press open. Arrange the braids, three colors of rickrack, and one strip of the satin cord on the shoulder area. The trims should have only a scant ⅛" between them. Begin with red rickrack tucked under one side of ⅞" braid, ⅝" braid, green rickrack tucked under one side of a ⅞" braid, satin cord, ⅜" braid, and 1" braid with yellow rickrack tucked under the far edge. The trims should be centered lengthwise over the shoulder seam.

3 Using the clear invisible thread to eliminate thread color changes, stitch each side of the braids with a narrow zigzag stitch. Use a braid foot on your machine, if available, to sew the satin cord. To help guide the cord, fit it through the hole in the presser foot. Use a zigzag stitch wide enough so the needle does not pierce the cord.

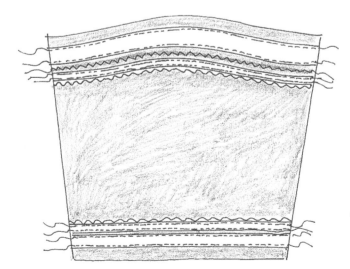

4 Stitch a ⅞" braid lengthwise on the top of each sleeve. Make sure the braid is placed ¼" from the seam allowance. The braid will have to be eased slight-

ly. Next, sew a strip of satin cord as in step #3. Lastly, sew a ⅝" braid with the green rickrack tucked under the far side.

5 At the sleeve edge, stitch a ⅞" braid lengthwise across the bottom of the sleeve. Make sure that the braid is placed ¾" away from the edge to allow for the placement of the binding. Next, stitch a ⅝" braid, with the yellow rickrack tucked under the edge closest to the shoulder.

6 Stitch the sleeves to the jacket with right sides together.

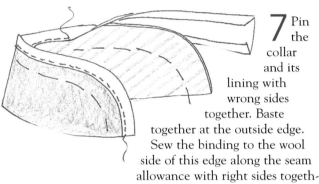

7 Pin the collar and its lining with wrong sides together. Baste together at the outside edge. Sew the binding to the wool side of this edge along the seam allowance with right sides together. Clip curves and fold the binding to the lining side. Pin and "stitch in the ditch" (along the actual seam) from the right side. Trim off excess binding close to the stitching on the lining side.

8 With right sides together, stitch the unbound collar edge to the neck edge, centering the collar on the center back of the jacket. Clip curves.

9 Draw an 8½" wide by 7" long rectangle on the right jacket front. The rectangle should begin ¾" from the top edge of the front flap corner and ¾" from the long side edge. Measure down 7", and draw a line with a chalk pencil. Return to the top of the line, measure over 8½", and draw a straight line. This line does not follow the neckline curve of the jacket. Draw a 7" line down and another 8½" line across to complete the rectangle.

10 Cut two 8" long pieces of ⅞" braid. Place one piece of braid ¾" from one of the 7" lines. Stitch along the outside edge of the braid with a narrow zigzag stitch. Stitch along the inside of the braid with red rickrack tucked underneath. Repeat with the other piece of braid on the other side.

11 Place the outside edge of a ⅝" braid along the drawn lines of the rectangle and zigzag stitch the inner edges of the braid only, mitering the corners. The raw edges of the ⅝" braid will be covered.

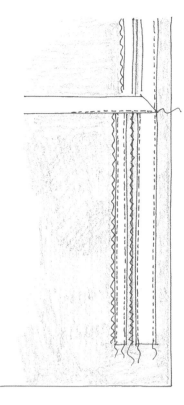

12 Stitch the 1" braid down the front of the jacket. The top of the braid is placed under the ⅝" braid rectangle and stitched ¾" from the long side edge. It should end 1¼" from the bottom edge of the jacket. Sew a strip of the satin cord next to it, and then a ⅝" braid with yellow rickrack tucked under the far side. All should end 1¼" from the hem edge. Now you can zigzag stitch around the outside of the ⅝" braid on the above rectangle.

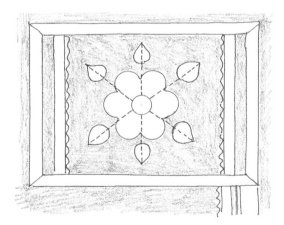

13 Trace the appliqué shapes onto the paper backing of the fusible web. Remove the liner on the other side and press the web to the wrong side of the wool felt. Cut out a flower from the red wool felt, six leaves from the green wool felt, and a flower center from the gold

wool felt. Center the red flower in the rectangle and press. Place the six leaves around the flower. Each leaf should be ⅝" from the side of each petal. Press.

14 With light green embroidery thread, straight stitch lines through the flower and each leaf. If your machine has a hand quilting stitch built in, this is a perfect time to use it. Begin stitching approximately ¼" from the point of each leaf to the edge of the flower. With gold embroidery thread, stitch lines from the end of the green stitching, across the flower to the other side. Press the gold center on the flower center.

15 Sew the underarm seam with right sides together.

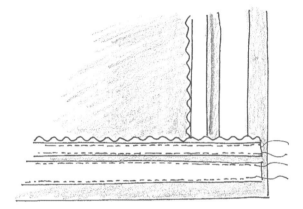

16 Stitch a ⅝" braid along the hem edge of the jacket fronts and back, ¾" away from the hem edge to accommodate the binding. Next, stitch the ⅝" braid with the red rickrack tucked under the far edge.

17 Sew the lining together at the shoulders and the underarm seam. Pin the right side of the neck edge of the jacket to the right side of the neck edge of the lining. Stitch, clip curves, trim seam allowances, and turn to the right side. Place the sleeve linings into the sleeves. Baste the front edges, the sleeve edges, and the hem of the lining and jacket together.

18 Sew the binding to the sleeve edges using the technique in step #7. Overlap the edges, tucking one edge under at the seam line.

19 Sew the binding to the front and hem edges of the jacket using the same technique as in step #7, mitering the corner at the hem edge.

20 Sew each side of the fastener to the top of the front opening of the jacket. Evenly space the other two fasteners along the front opening and sew each side.

Scandinavian Jacket Appliqués

Leaf

Flower
Center

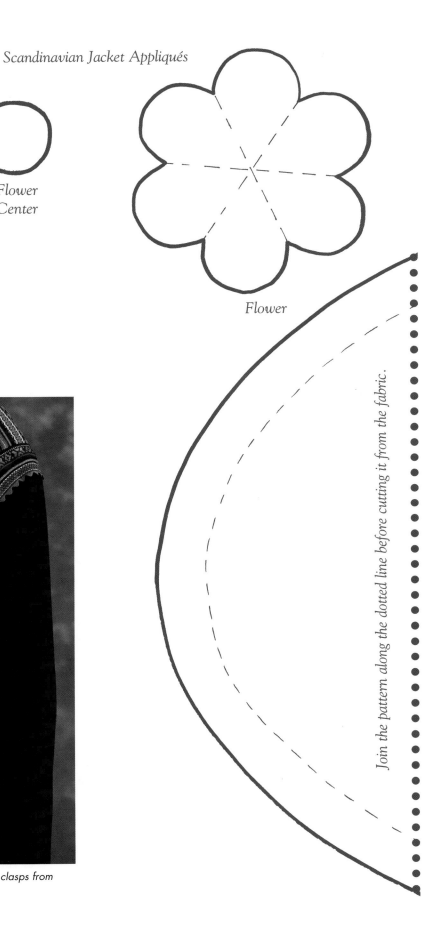

Flower

Join the pattern along the dotted line before cutting it from the fabric.

The Scandinavian Jacket is accented by pewter clasps from Scandinavia.

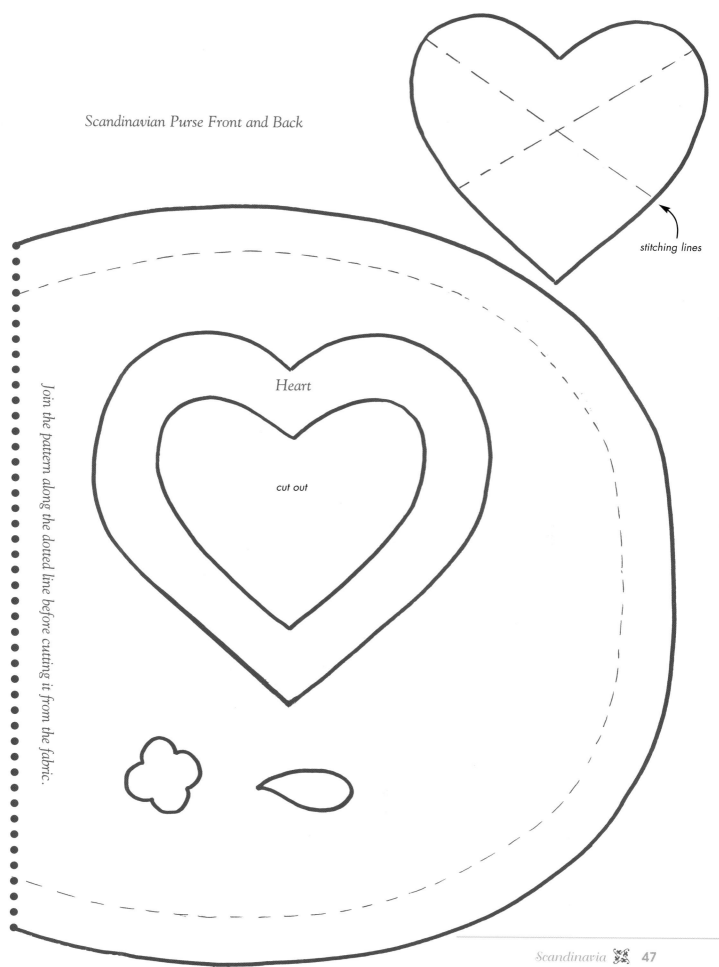

Scandinavian Purse Front and Back

stitching lines

Heart

cut out

Join the pattern along the dotted line before cutting it from the fabric.

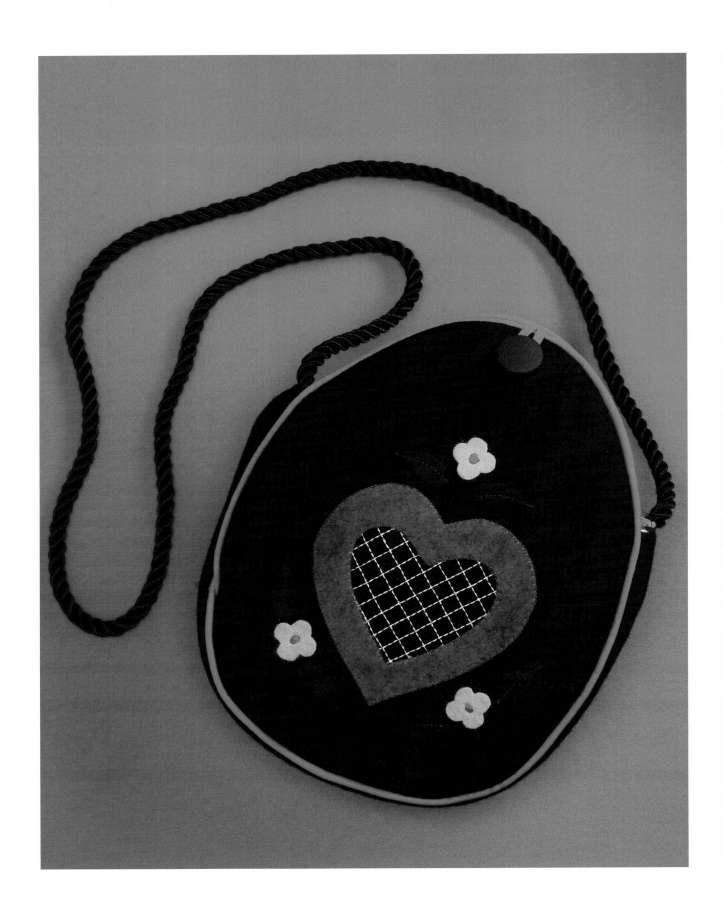

Scandinavian Purse

Supplies:

- ½ yd. black medium weight wool fabric
- ½ yd. cotton print for lining
- ½ yd. red broadcloth for piping
- ½ yd. medium to heavy weight fusible interfacing
- 60" cording, ⅛" wide
- 3" squares each of gold and green wool felt
- 6" square of red wool felt
- Fusible web for appliqués
- White and red machine embroidery thread
- Black button, ⅞"
- 1¼ yd. black cord for strap, ⅜"

Since women's costumes from Norway and Sweden do not have pockets, there is often a "hanging pocket" or purse attached to the belt in front. A silver hook clips over the belt and a silver purse frame attaches to it. The purse is made of fabric from the costume and is embroidered with similar motifs. The filling stitches inside the floral and circular motifs resemble open latticework.

The purse designed here is a shoulder purse with a strap, which makes it a practical addition to any wardrobe. The purse maintains the Scandinavian oval shape with a button closure at the top. The heart and floral appliqués are made from the same wool felt as the Scandinavian Jacket. The filling stitch inside the heart is sewn with white machine embroidery thread using a reinforced machine straight stitch.

All seam allowances are ½".

1 Cut out a purse front, back, and a 3" x 19½" strip for the gusset from the black wool, lining, and interfacing. Fuse the interfacing to the wrong side of the black wool pieces.

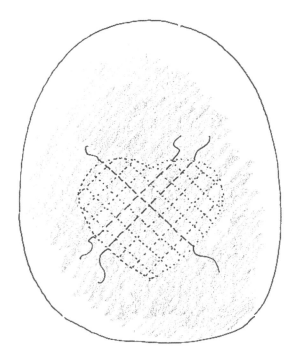

2 Center the heart template on the purse front 2" from the bottom edge. Draw the outline and the two diagonal lines inside the heart with a chalk pencil, as shown on the pattern piece (page 47). With white machine embroidery thread, stitch along one of the diagonal lines. Use a reinforced straight stitch (each stitch is stitched twice) if your machine has it, or use a 3.5 length straight stitch. Move to one side, a presser foot width over from the first row, and stitch a second row. Continue stitching rows of straight stitches inside the heart until it is filled completely. Turn the fabric and stitch the other drawn diagonal line. Move one presser foot width over as before and stitch rows of straight stitches until the heart is completely filled. Do not stitch around the outline of the heart.

3 Trace the heart, three flowers, and six leaves (page 47) onto the paper side of the fusible web. Peel off the other side and stick the heart to the red felt, the flowers to the gold felt, and the leaves to the green felt. Cut out the motifs.

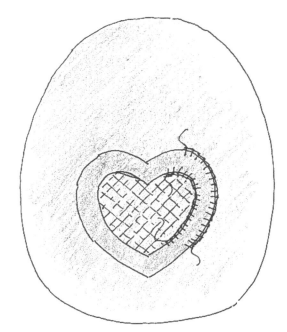

4 Place the heart over the stitching so that the outline drawn on the black wool is covered. Using red machine embroidery thread, stitch around the inside and outside of the red heart with a narrow machine blanket stitch or zigzag stitch. If you prefer, the blanket stitch can be worked by hand.

5 Press the flowers and leaves in place around the heart, as shown. With red machine embroidery thread, stitch the center of each flower with a satin zigzag stitch. With green sewing thread, stitch the center of each leaf to attach to the fabric. Pull the tails of the green thread to the backside and knot.

6 Cut 1½" bias strips for the piping. Fold the bias over the cording, and sew close to the cord using a piping foot or zipper foot on the sewing machine. Trim the seam allowance of the piping to ½" if necessary.

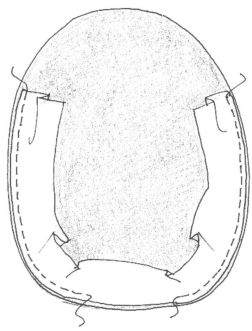

9 Sew the gusset lining to the front lining. Sew the gusset to the back lining, leaving an 8" opening along the bottom.

10 For the button loop, cut a ½" x 1½" bias strip of red fabric. Press the long sides ⅛" to the wrong side. Press each side again so that the folded edges meet, and slipstitch. Place the cut edges of the strip along the seam allowance of the top center of the back purse. Baste.

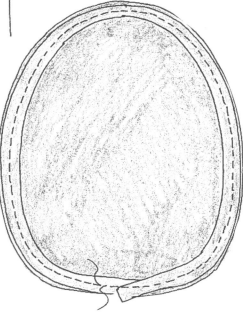

7 Stitch the piping to the front purse, overlapping the ends in the seam allowance. Repeat with the back purse.

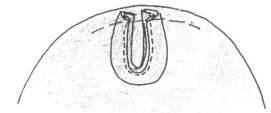

11 Place the ends of the black cord along the seam allowance at the top of the gusset, and baste.

12 With right sides together, sew the lining to the purse around the front, gusset tops, and the back. Turn to the right side through the opening at the bottom of the lining. Press the gusset side of the opening ½" to the wrong side, and slipstitch closed.

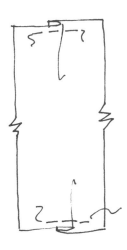

8 Make a pleat at the top of the wool gusset and the lining gusset so that it measures 2½" and baste across the top. With right sides together, center the gusset along the bottom of the purse front. The gusset will extend approximately two-thirds up each side. Stitch the gusset to the back with right sides together.

13 Sew the button to the center of the purse front, ⅞" from the top of the purse.

Western Europe

Western Europe has a long tradition of embroidery and folk art. Folk costume in Europe generally refers to peasant-style clothing. For women in most areas, it consists of a blouse and many layers of skirts. These are topped with a fitted bodice or sleeveless vest and a beautifully decorated apron that concentrates the most elaborate part of the ensemble in front where it is most visible. Men commonly wear jackets and breeches. Each small region developed its own style of embroideries, patterns, and colors. Most of us are familiar with the *lederhosen* of Bavaria, the short leather trousers with embroidered suspenders, and the *dirndl* of Germany and Austria, a full petticoat skirt.

The embellishment used in Western Europe was embroidery. The most common methods were whitework, drawn fabric, and cutwork. Flax and wool are most often used for fabrics and threads. Silk was introduced in the sixth century. Universal decorative motifs include stylized flowers, birds, trees of life, and hearts. Samplers, a method for testing your embroidery skills with a wide variety of techniques, began in the seventeenth century and quickly spread throughout Europe. "Berlin wool work," which was done with tent or cross stitches worked on a single weave canvas with wool, gained popularity in the nineteenth century. The colorful designs published throughout the western world were mainly floral or pictorial scenes.

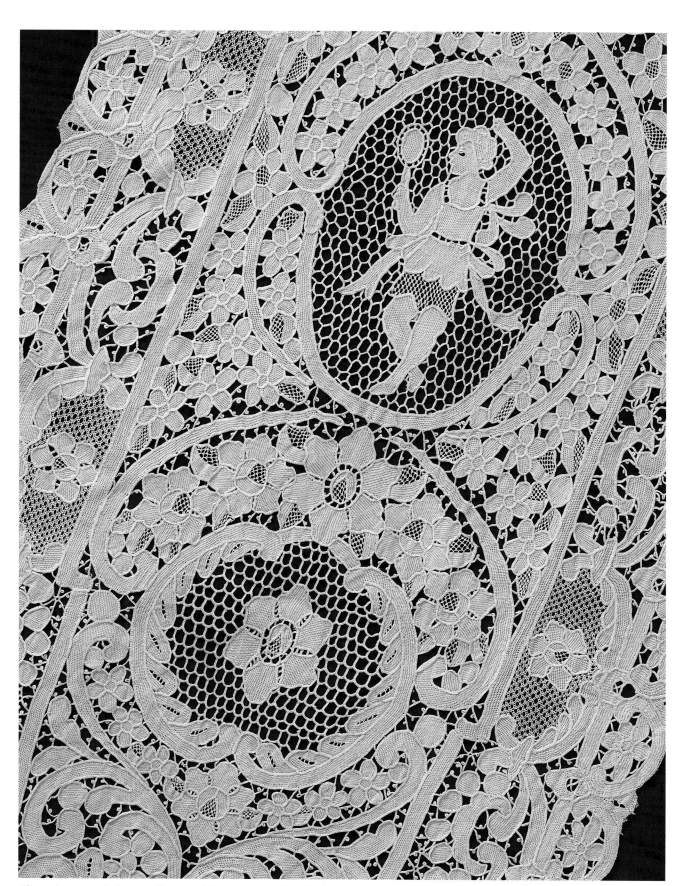

Shown here is an Italian needle lace table runner from the Glensheen collection in Duluth, Minnesota.

English Tea Cozy

Supplies:

- 1½ yd. linen or linen/cotton blend
- 1 yd. cording, ¼" wide
- ½ yd. lace edging, 1¾" wide
- ½ yd. lace edging, 1¼" wide
- 1 yd. lace insertion, ¾" wide
- Corner of napkin or hankie with embroidery or cutwork
- ¼ yd. lace edging, ⅝" wide
- ½ yd. thin cotton batting
- Tear-away stabilizer
- Fine sewing thread to match fabric

The British Isles is known for its many varieties of intricate whitework embroidery. Ayrshire whitework, with embroidered satin stitches, stem stitch, and cut out designs, was so delicate it looked like lace. It was developed in Scotland. Coggeshall work, a tamboured chain stitch that is stitched to a muslin background, is named after a village in Essex. Other forms of whitework flourished in Ireland. Carrickmacross work is embroidered linen stitched over net with the outside of the design cut away to reveal the net underneath.

This ecru linen and lace tea cozy is reminiscent of whitework. The embroidered cutwork motif used in the center of the tea cozy is a corner of a napkin given to me by my mother. The napkin was stained, so I did not use it. You can also use handkerchiefs that have been passed down from other family members or picked up at yard sales. The delicate cotton lace is stitched to the linen background using entredeux created on the sewing machine. Entredeux, which means "between the two," is a strip of embroidered cotton that resembles a ladder. It was traditionally used to join fabric to lace. If you do not have the stitch built into your machine, you can stitch the laces to the fabric with a zigzag stitch.

All seam allowances are ½".

1 Using the pattern piece, cut four tea cozy covers from the linen or linen-cotton blend. Two will be used for the lining. Cut a 1½" x 33" bias strip from the fabric for the piping, piecing if necessary.

2 Cut the corner of the napkin/hankie so that the design is centered and the sides extend up 4¾". Pin the wrong side of the corner of the napkin/hankie over tear-away stabilizer. Place the ⅝" lace just inside one of the bottom edges of the corner. Stitch with a built-in entredeux stitch to attach the lace to the fabric of the napkin/hankie. If your machine doesn't have an entredeux stitch, use a medium-width close zigzag stitch. Stitch the lace along one side until you reach the corner.

Miter the lace at the corner and continue stitching along the other side. Tear away the stabilizer.

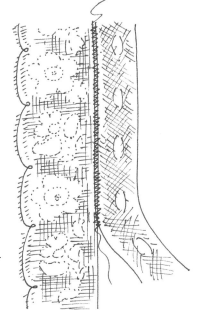

3 Cut the lace insertion and the 1¼" lace edging 16" long. Place the straight side of the edging and one of the sides of the insertion together under the presser foot. Using a medium-width zigzag stitch, stitch the laces together. Cut in half to make two 8" pieces.

4 Place the napkin/hankie corner on the center of one of the fabric covers so that the top edge is flush with the cover's top edge. Pin the stabilizer under the napkin/hankie and fabric. Using the entredeux stitch or a close zigzag stitch, sew the lace insertion side of one of the 8" strips to a long side of the napkin/hankie. You will stitch over the napkin/hankie, fabric, and stabilizer until you reach the end of the lace. Repeat with the other side. Tear away the stabilizer. Trim any fabric from the napkin/hankie that extends under the lace and may be seen.

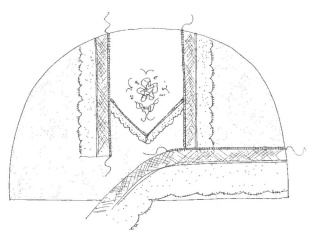

5 Stitch the wide lace edging to the remaining lace insertion, using the same technique as in step #3. Place the lace strip horizontally over the ends of the 8" lace strips, and stitch, using the entredeux stitch or a close zigzag stitch. Be sure that the stabilizer is under the stitching. Tear away the stabilizer.

6 Cut two tea cozy covers from the batting. Baste ⅜" from all the edges of the front cover and another cover that will be used for the back. Trim the seam.

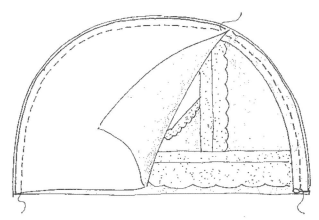

7 Fold the wrong side of 1½" bias strip around the cording and stitch close to the cording to create piping. Stitch the piping on the curved edge only of the front cover along the seam line.

8 With right sides together, stitch the back cover to the front cover along the curved edge only. Clip the curves, trim the seam allowances, and turn to the right side. Press.

9 Sew the remaining lining covers with right sides together along the curved edge, leaving a 10" opening in the top of the covers. Clip the curves and trim the seam. Place the right side of the lining over the right side of the cover and stitch along the straight bottom edge. Trim the seam and turn to the right side through the opening in the lining. Pin the seam allowances of the opening to the wrong side, and stitch the opening closed. Press the seam at the bottom edge so that the lining is inside. If desired, slip-stitch by hand the top of the lining to the inside of the tea cozy to keep the lining from slipping out.

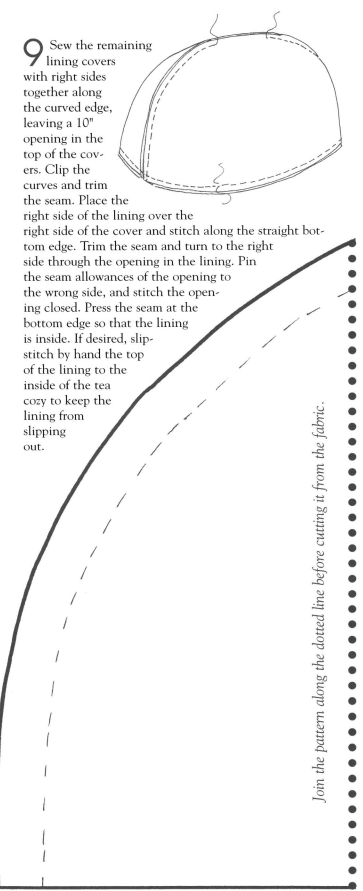

Join the pattern along the dotted line before cutting it from the fabric.

English Tea Cozy

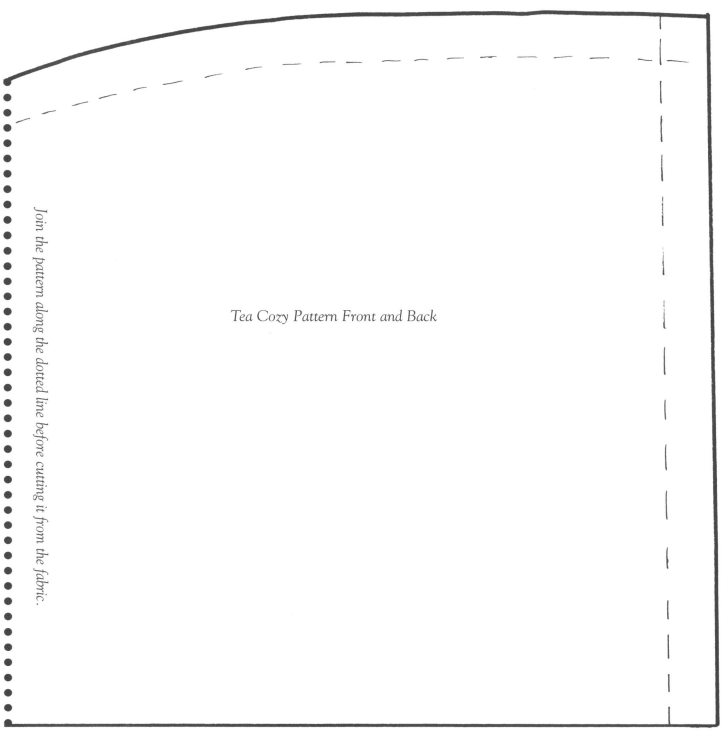

Tea Cozy Pattern Front and Back

Join the pattern along the dotted line before cutting it from the fabric.

Place on fold

The German Sweater-Jacket with Floral Embroidery is worn by Sue Anderson.

German Sweater-Jacket with Floral Embroidery

Supplies:

- Purchased wool or "boiled wool" sweater or jacket with princess seams and buttons fastening in front
- 3-stranded tapestry wool in 32" lengths (approximate amounts):
  - 6 of white
  - 4 of light yellow
  - 3 of pale gray
  - 9 of medium blue
  - 9 of light blue
  - 6 of medium green
  - 1 of light green
- Large-eyed crewel needle, such as a #1 or #3
- Paper for tracing

Folk costume in Germany is well known. The *dirndl* and leather *lederhosen* are the most common. These items are heavily embroidered with stylized flowers, such as edelweiss or blue gentian. Oak leaves are also popular. *Loden*, a waterproof wool cloth that has been fulled (the fibers are treated with water and heat to make them compact), stretched, and dried, developed in the alpine regions and is still made today. The adoption in the 1960s of the *loden*, a gray wool suit with green trim and many metal buttons, has continued these traditions.

This sweater-jacket continues the tradition of wool embroidery with floral designs. I chose to stitch the embroidery on a "boiled wool" sweater (the knitted fibers have been compacted) that has princess-style seams and metal buttons, commonly seen in folk clothing. The wool I used for stitching is tapestry wool, a three-stranded yarn often sold by the cut strands. The alpine flower motifs, edelweiss and forget-me-nots, are stitched between the buttons on the front of the sweater. If you prefer, you can stitch the same motifs on a fabric jacket.

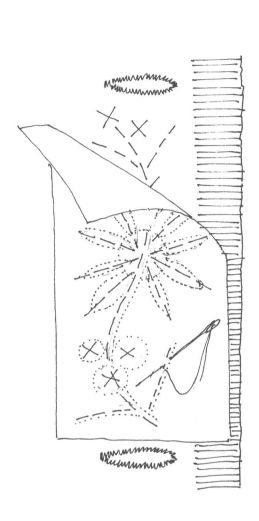

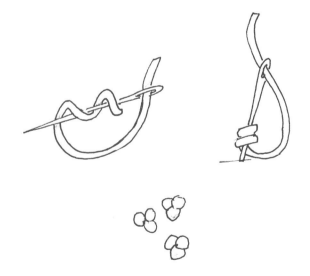

2 Work the design with only one strand of wool. Begin working lazy daisy stitches (known as detached chain stitch) with the white wool for the edelweiss. Stitch a long straight stitch in the center of the each lazy daisy stitch.

1 Trace the pattern used between the buttons onto tracing paper. Pin the pattern between the buttons and baste the flower shapes and the vine and leaf lines with sewing thread. Your design may need to be lengthened or shortened depending on the distances between the buttonholes. Tear off the paper. Repeat with all the other spaces. Note that I varied the color and placement of the forget-me-knots in each motif for interest. You can choose to work them all the same if you prefer.

3 Fill the center with French knots using both the yellow and gray wool, randomly placing the colors.

4 Work the stem with the stem stitch and medium green wool. The leaves are worked next. The leaf is two rows of the same stem stitch, with the medium green wool stitched first and the light green wool stitched above it.

5 The forget-me-knots are a cluster of five French knots in two shades of blue with a yellow French knot in the center. Work them over the stem, following the pattern.

6 Trace the design for the top and bottom edges of the sweater onto tracing paper. Pin the pattern on the top and bottom edges of the right side of the sweater, as shown in the photo. Baste the French knot placement and the vine and leaf lines with sewing thread. Tear off the paper. Pin the pattern on the top and bottom edges of the left side of the sweater and baste the placement lines. Tear off the paper.

7 Work the stem, leaves, and forget-me-knots on each side of the top and bottom of the center front.

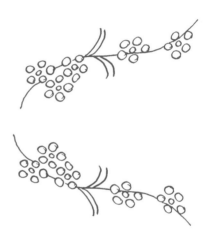

Design for top and bottom on left side

Embroidery Design placed between buttons

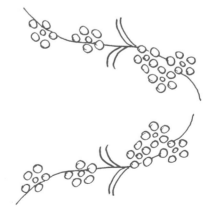

Design for top and bottom on right side

Costumes and folk art from Eastern Europe are highly ornamented. It has been said that some of the most beautiful styles and designs are due to the merging of the East and the West, combining the best of both worlds. The bodice of a woman's costume is a long shift or gown, due to Asian influence, instead of the shorter blouse from Western Europe. Both full and narrow skirts are worn with short or long sleeveless vests. In Russia, a pinafore dress hanging with shoulder straps, called a sarafan, is worn over a homespun shift.

A man's costume consists of lavishly embroidered jackets and breeches. The breeches in the southern areas tend to be wider, showing a Turkish influence. Sheepskin is a common material used for vests and jackets, including the Hungarian szur, and is appliquéd with leather.

Red is the most often used color in embroidery, stitched on a natural linen background. Counted thread work is the most popular, but metal thread work, cutwork, and appliqué are also embellishment techniques used in the area. In Armenia and Russia, freshwater pearls and precious stones are stitched to silk or velvet.

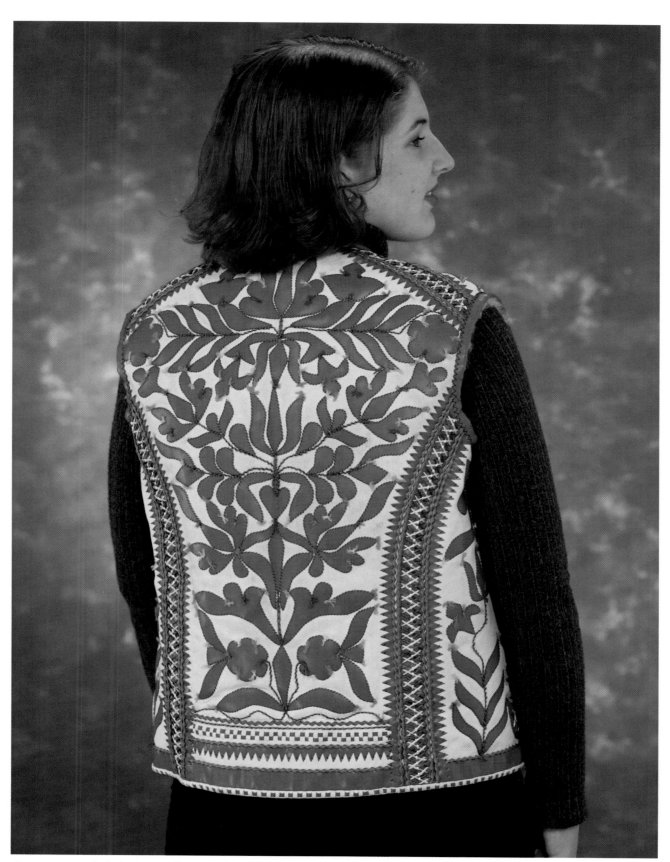

Opposite page: Cathy Nelson's collection includes this woman's cap with incredible weaving and embroidery. This page: Back of sheep-skin vest from Slovakia.

Stina Lapaugh wears the Slovakian Appliqued Vest.

Slovakian Appliquéd Vest

Supplies:

- Vest pattern with a stand-up collar and princess-style seams in the front and the back*
- Cream heavyweight cotton flannel
- Coordinating print cotton fabric for lining
- 4" x 11" piece of light brown Ultrasuede®
- 4" x 14" piece of dark brown Ultrasuede
- ⅛ yd. tan Ultrasuede
- 2 packages medium red rickrack
- 1 package narrow red rickrack
- 2 skeins moss green embroidery floss
- 1 skein red embroidery floss
- 1 package light brown double-folded bias tape
- 4 leather-look buttons, ⅞"
- 12" of red tubular bias tape
- Clear invisible thread
- Temporary spray adhesive
- Red machine embroidery thread

*I used Butterick #6741.

While women wear beautiful embroidered vests, aprons, and many-layered skirts, men make sheepskin vests and coats with the wooly side in and the leather side out. Intricate leather appliqué, leather buttons, and embroidery are added for decoration. One version features red appliqués applied to natural suede, but others may have different colors. The appliqués are in heart and floral shapes.

One interesting decorative embellishment is the use of "wolves' teeth" along the edges of the coats and vests. These are small pyramid-shaped appliqués that are thought to protect the wearer from evil that may enter through the openings.

The vest adapts well to a modern wardrobe. I have sewn mine with a heavy cream-colored flannel rather than sheepskin. The appliqués are made from Ultrasuede®. The stitching around the appliqués is done with a machine stitch that resembles a blanket stitch, but it can be zigzag stitched instead. I have placed rickrack under the trims along the edges. Only the pointed pyramid shapes that peek out are reminiscent of wolves' teeth. When you wear this vest, you can be assured that you are safe from harm!

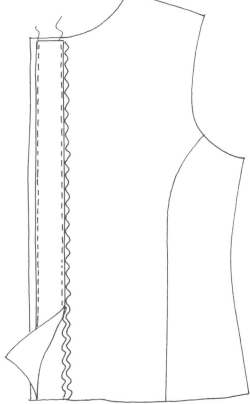

1 Cut out the fronts, side fronts, back, side backs, and collar for the vest from the cream flannel, trimming off the seam allowances along the center fronts and the armholes. Trim off the hem of the vest. Cut out the same pieces from the cotton lining fabric.

2 With right sides together, sew each front to the side fronts. Press the seam allowances open.

3 Trace the stems and appliqué placement on each front with a washout marker.

4 Cut two 1¼" strips of tan Ultrasuede the length of the center fronts. Spray the wrong side of one of the strips with temporary spray adhesive. Place a strip along the center front ⅝" from the center front edge, tucking the medium rickrack under the inside edge so that approximately one-half of it peeks out. Using the clear invisible thread, stitch the Ultrasuede and rickrack to the fabric with a narrow zigzag stitch. Repeat with the other side.

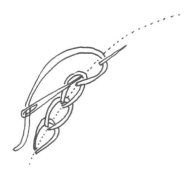

5 Using all six strands of the green embroidery floss, work chain stitches for the stems by hand on each vest front.

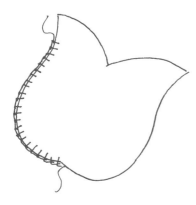

6 Cut out four tulip shapes from the dark brown Ultrasuede, two flower shapes from the light brown Ultrasuede, and four ovals from the tan Ultrasuede. Spray the wrong side of each appliqué with adhesive and press into place. Using the red machine embroidery thread, stitch a narrow blanket stitch by machine around each appliqué. If you do not have the blanket stitch on your machine, use a narrow zigzag stitch.

7 With all six strands of red embroidery floss, stitch small backstitches above the tulips and ovals as marked on the pattern piece.

8 Trace the stems and appliqué placement on the back of the vest. The lower ends of the stems should be placed 4½" from the lower edge of the vest. With the green floss, embroider chain stitches along the stems as on the front.

9 Cut two flower shapes from the dark brown Ultrasuede, one tulip shape from the light brown Ultrasuede, and two ovals from the tan Ultrasuede. Spray the wrong side of the appliqués with the adhesive and press in place. Stitch blanket stitches with the red machine embroidery around the edges of the appliqués. Stitch the backstitches above the tulip and ovals with red embroidery floss, as on the front.

10 Cut a 1¼" strip of tan Ultrasuede long enough to fit across the back over the ends of the stems. Spray the wrong side with adhesive, and place it over the ends of the stems, tucking in the medium rickrack on each side. Stitch with clear invisible thread using a narrow zigzag on each side of the strip.

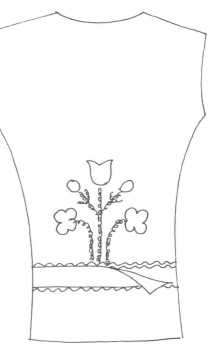

11 Stitch the back to the fronts of the vest, and sew the side seams according to the pattern instructions. Attach the collar to the vest, tucking in medium rickrack in the seam so that half of the rickrack peeks out from the seam.

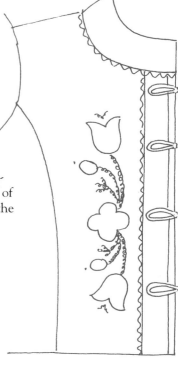

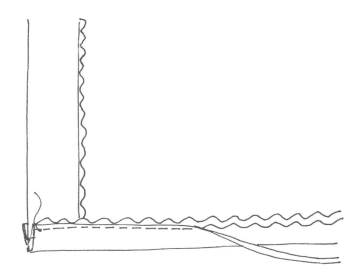

12 Cut the tubular bias tape in four equal pieces to make button loops. Fold each in half, and place the cut edges on the seam line of the right vest front. The first loop should be placed just under the collar, and the others are equally spaced down the front. With right sides together, sew the lining to the vest along the center fronts and the top edge of the collar. Be sure to avoid catching the Ultrasuede in the stitching. Turn to the right side and press.

13 Using the clear invisible thread, topstitch along the Ultrasuede very close to the center front edge so that the edge will lie flat.

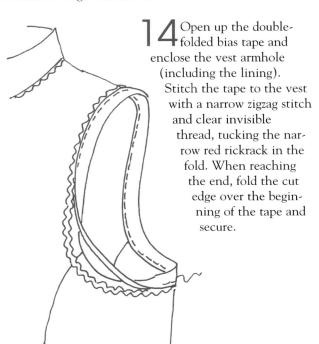

14 Open up the double-folded bias tape and enclose the vest armhole (including the lining). Stitch the tape to the vest with a narrow zigzag stitch and clear invisible thread, tucking the narrow red rickrack in the fold. When reaching the end, fold the cut edge over the beginning of the tape and secure.

15 Enclose the hem of the vest in the double-folded bias tape, and stitch a narrow zigzag stitch with the clear invisible thread, tucking the medium rickrack in the fold. Be sure to fold the raw edges under at each center front.

16 Sew the buttons to the left front edge.

Back view of the Slovakian Appliqued Vest.

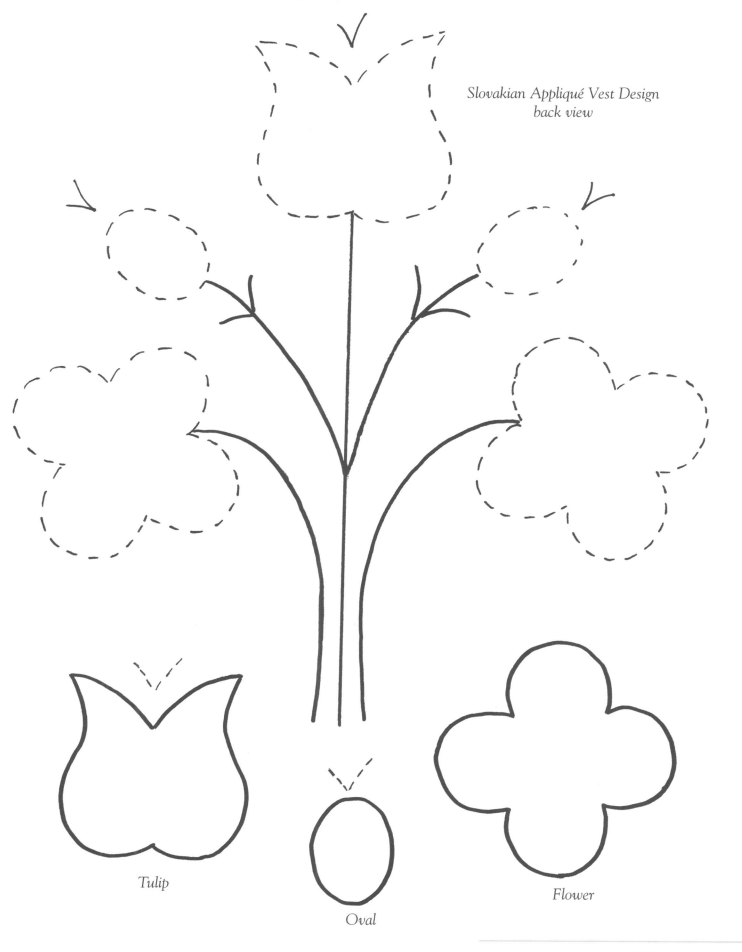

Slovakian Appliqué Vest Design
back view

Tulip

Oval

Flower

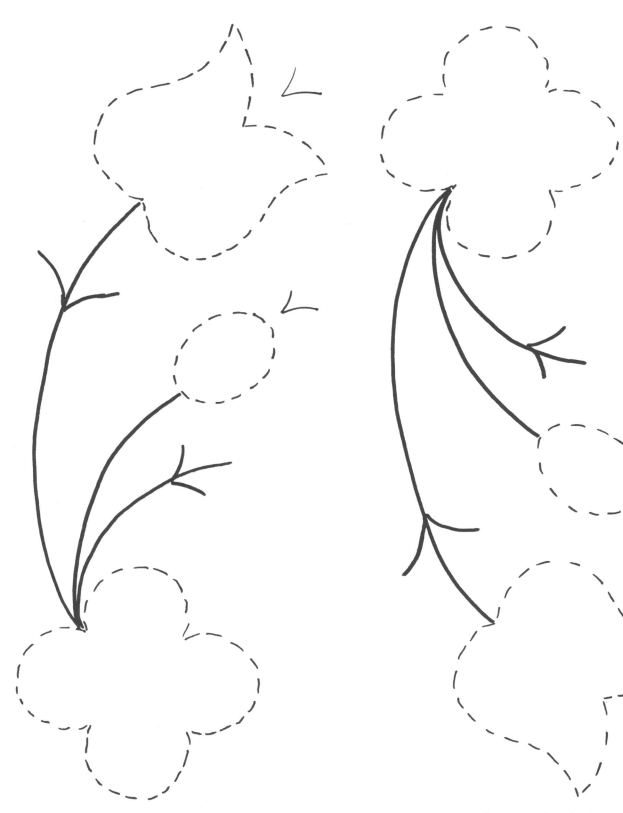

Slovakian Appliqué Vest
Upper right side design
(The center flower overlaps onto the center
flower on the lower design.
Reverse both for the left side.)

Lower right side design

Hungarian Feltwork Jacket

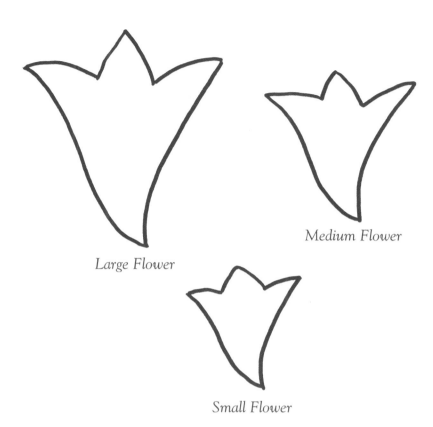

Large Flower

Medium Flower

Small Flower

Stem for lapel

Stem for sleeve

The Hungarian Feltwork Jacket is worn by Mary Beth Tarnowski.

Hungarian Feltwork Jacket

Supplies:

- Purchased red wool blazer
- ½ yd. black wool felt
- Fusible tape, ¼" wide
- Temporary spray adhesive
- Black sewing thread

Hungarian shepherds wore a *szur*, a heavy woolen waterproof coat, for centuries. The decorated *szur* was worn for courting and weddings. It was even draped over the wearer's coffin. Decoration began with satin stitch embroidery in stylized floral and bird motifs. Red was the color for lower nobility with black worn by the shepherds. The embroidery almost disappeared in the nineteenth century with the advent of the sewing machine. Colored fabric, and eventually felt, was layered and applied in large pieces. The designs were stitched quickly by machine and cut out with tiny scissors.

Felt appliqué is still done in Hungary today for a variety of decorative items. Red, white, and black are the most common colors. Designs are drawn on the felt backing. A second layer is added and stitched by machine. The piece is turned over and the design is cut with chisels.

I have trimmed a purchased ready-made blazer with felt appliqués. The thin pointed trim along the collar and pocket edges is cut with pinking shears instead of a chisel. The floral appliqués are cut out along the outside only and then stitched to the blazer. The inside is carefully cut out along the stitching lines.

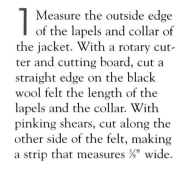

1 Measure the outside edge of the lapels and collar of the jacket. With a rotary cutter and cutting board, cut a straight edge on the black wool felt the length of the lapels and the collar. With pinking shears, cut along the other side of the felt, making a strip that measures ⅜" wide.

2 Stick the fusible tape to the wrong side of the felt strip. Place the strip along the jacket just inside the outer edge of the lapels and collar. Press into place. The ends of the strip will tuck under the front of the jacket. Stitch with a 3.0 straight stitch down the center of the felt strip.

3 For the lapels, cut out a large flower, two medium flowers, and two small flowers (page 71) from black wool felt. Turn the flower pattern pieces over and cut out again. Cut out a stem, turn the pattern piece over, and cut out again. You may have to lengthen or shorten the stem depending on the size of your lapel.

4 Pin the large flowers at the top of the lapels. Pin the straight end of the stem under the large flower. Curve the stem downward, following the illustration and pinning the medium flowers on each side. Pin the two small flowers on each side of the stem, ending near the curved bottom of the stem.

5 When placement is completed, spray the temporary spray adhesive on the wrong side of the stem and stick the stem on the jacket. Using a straight stitch, stitch down the center of the stem. Spray the temporary spray adhesive on the wrong side of the large flower, and stick it to the jacket. Stitch with straight stitches a scant ⅛" from the edge. The stitches should be evenly spaced from the edge of the flower, but do not have to be exact. With sharp pointed scissors, cut out the center

a scant ⅛" from the stitching. Be careful not to cut into the jacket. It is easier to stitch the flowers in place before the centers are cut.

6 Repeat with the other flowers.

7 Repeat steps #4-6 on the other lapel, but make sure that the placement is a mirror image of the first side.

8 If desired, the pockets can be decorated. Cut strips as in step #1, and make them long enough to go around the pockets. Fuse and stitch around each pocket. Cut three medium flowers from felt with the pattern piece. Turn the pattern piece over and cut three more. Place three flowers above each pocket so that the points at the bottom of the flowers point outward. Stitch and cut as in step #5. Repeat with the remaining flowers on the other side.

9 For the sleeves, cut two small flowers and one stem from felt using the pattern piece. Turn the pattern piece over and cut again.

10 Curve the stem on the center of the sleeve edge as shown in the illustration, pinning a flower on each side of the stem. When placement is completed, spray the wrong side of the pieces and stick them to the jacket. Stitch and cut as in step #5. Repeat with the remaining stem and flowers on the other sleeve. Be sure the placement is a mirror image of the first sleeve.

Close-up of the Hungarian Feltwork.

The Jacket with Polish Parzenica Trim is worn by Char Harkins.

Jacket with Polish Parzenica Trim

Supplies:

- Purchased tweed zippered front jacket
- 2⅔ yd. nubby black braid, ⅜" wide
- 2⅔ yd. red braid, ⅛" wide
- Purchased red tassel, 1½" long
- Tracing or tissue paper
- Red and black sewing threads

Like other European countries, Poland has many colorful embroidered costumes for both men and women. One unusual embroidery detail on men's breeches is called *parzenica*. This elaborate stitching is done on the two front openings at the waist and occasionally along both sides of the slits at the ankles of the trouser legs. It runs vertically along each side and around the bottom of the openings. Brightly colored wool or commercial braid is couched or stitched using satin, chain, or herringbone stitches that are unique to each village. Up to seven colors can be used in the embroidery. The motifs are circular or heart-shaped with loops.

I have chosen to incorporate this type of embellishment on a boxy style of jacket. The linear *parzenica* is not applied to an opening, but instead it is applied on the front of the jacket in four places. The length of the *parzenica* can be adjusted if necessary to accommodate all sizes. I chose two colors of braid that were basted first for placement and then zigzag stitched permanently with clear invisible thread. You could also work this type of embroidery around pocket openings.

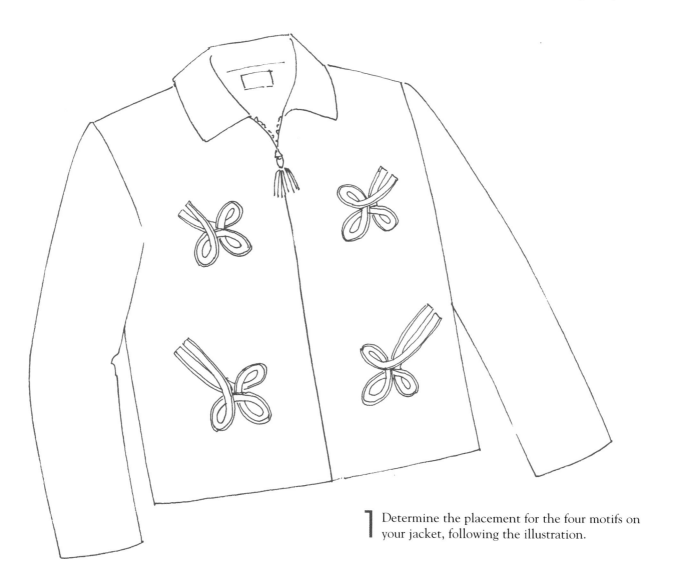

1 Determine the placement for the four motifs on your jacket, following the illustration.

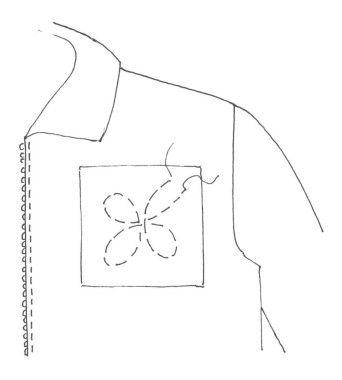

4 Continue basting the black and red braids over the stitching lines of the motif. Be sure that the braids cross over each other as shown in the illustration. Turn the ends under at the end of the motif.

5 Using matching thread and a medium-width zigzag stitch, stitch the black braid to the jacket. Float the thread over the red braid as you stitch the motif. Stitch the red braid with matching thread, floating the thread over the black braid. Trim all threads when completed.

6 Baste the small motif, drawn on tissue paper, to the right side of the jacket. Tear away the tissue paper. Begin with the black braid at the right side of the top of the motif, so that the braids will cross in a mirror image of the other side. Stitch as above.

7 Baste the larger motif, drawn on tissue paper, to the lower left side of the jacket. Begin with the black braid on the left side of the motif as done with the smaller motif on the left side. Stitch as above.

8 Repeat step #6, but with the larger motif.

9 Attach the tassel to the zipper pull.

2 Trace the smaller motif onto tissue or tracing paper. Place the tracing on the left side of the jacket and baste over the stitching lines. Use contrasting thread and large stitches. Tear away the tissue paper.

3 Begin with black braid by turning the end under slightly at the left side of the top of the motif. Baste over the stitching lines with black thread around the first loop and stop. Turn the end of the red braid under slightly on the outside of the black braid. Next to the black braid, baste the red braid with red thread around the first loop, and stop.

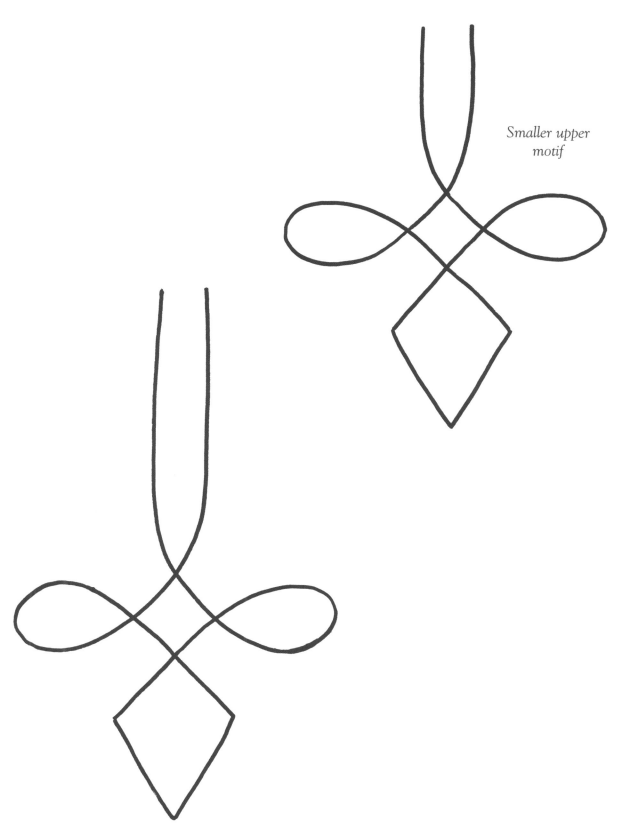

Smaller upper
motif

Larger lower motif

Russian Jeweled Frame

Supplies:

- 11" x 14" rectangle of aqua silk dupioni
- Unfinished picture frame with an opening size of 4" x 6" and an outside dimension of 6¾" x 8¾"
- Quilt batting
- 1 ball of #8 DMC perle cotton, color #519
- 1 package of #11 Toho round seed beads in cream opaque lustre
- 20 teardrop-shaped pearl beads, 9mm x 6mm
- 12 round pearl beads, 3mm
- #10 crochet hook
- #10 tapestry beading needle
- Spray adhesive
- Water-soluble fabric glue stick
- Lightweight iron-on interfacing
- Air erasable fabric marker
- Optional: Felt or Ultrasuede, to match the color of the silk dupioni
- White sewing thread

(Designed by Marilee Sagat)

Affluent Russian women wore a *sarafan*. This was a pinafore-type dress with shoulder straps constructed from beautiful silk brocaded fabric. A jeweled headdress for married women, called a *kokochniki*, and a *povoinik* for unmarried women was worn with this costume. It was made from stiffened cardboard, covered with silk or velvet, and adorned with embroidery and jewels, including freshwater pearls from Russian lakes and streams. They often had pearl fringe on the forehead. Each area had its own unique style.

Western Russia has a Christian heritage with elaborate vestments stitched for the church with silk, jewels, and threads embroidered on silk or velvet. Individual homes had embroidered icon covers as a religious focal point. Icons or treasured photos were often inserted in frames ornamented with tatting and jewels.

This jeweled frame consists of a flat-front wooden frame covered with batting and silk. The corners of the frame are embellished with crocheted, not tatted, motifs with pearls. The motifs are connected with a crocheted chain with beads added as you crochet. The trim is applied to the fabric before the frame is covered. Selecting a frame that has a narrow inside lip will make the frame easier to cover. If desired, you can make your own frame from cardboard covered with silk and batting.

Crocheted Embellishment

Note: *Before crocheting, transfer the beads onto crochet cotton. First string approximately 36 inches of the beads onto sewing thread. Make a slipknot at the end of the sewing thread and insert the perle cotton into the loop created by the slipknot. Slide the beads to the perle cotton.*

Gauge

A complete 12-chain Petal = ½" from base to beaded tip

Abbreviations:

ch = chain
sc = single crochet
sl st = slipstitch
sl bd ch = slide bead to the backside of the crochet hook, chain stitch
sl bd sc = slide bead to the backside of the crochet hook, single crochet

5–Petal Motif – Make 4

Ch 6, join to make loop.

Ch 1, sc in loop, ch 12, sc in loop*. Repeat from * to * 4 times for a total of 5 loops.

** Sl st into petal loop, ch 1, 6 sc in petal loop, sl bd sc 3 times, 6 sc in petal loop, sl st in center loop**. Repeat from ** to ** 4 more times. After last loop, end off. Weave in both loose ends.

3-Petal Motif with Beaded Connection

Beaded Connection: Ch 2, * sl bd ch, ch*. Repeat from * to * 9 more times (10 beads crocheted in place).

3-Petal Motif: ch 6, join in 6th ch from hook to form loop. Ch 1, TURN. Sc in center loop, ch 6, sc in center loop, ch 12, sc in center loop, ch 6, sc in center loop, TURN.

In first ch 6 petal, sl st into petal, ch 1, 3 sc, 3 sl bd sc, 3 sc, sl st into center loop.

In ch 12 petal, sl st into ch 12 petal, ch 1, 6 sc, 3 sl bd sc, 6 sc, sl st into center loop.

In last ch 6 petal, repeat first ch 6 petal step.

Repeat the beaded connection and 3-petal motif as many times as you like for each of the four sides of the frame. End each string with a beaded connection and end. DO NOT CUT beginning or ending thread.

Construction of Crochet Embellishment on the Silk Dupioni Fabric

1 Carefully lay all the beaded connections and 3-petal motif sections on the ironing board with bead side down, and lightly starch and steam press them to keep the section flat.

2 Take a 3-petal motif and beaded connection, and tie each end to a 5-petal motif in between two of the petals. Count two petals over and tie an end from another section between the second and third petals. Three of the five petals will be facing the inner corner of the frame (see photo). Continue this step until all 3-petal sections are connected to all of the 5-petal motifs. Set aside.

3 Cut a piece of interfacing the same size as the surface of the frame. Iron this interfacing onto the backside of the silk dupioni, following the manufacturer's instructions.

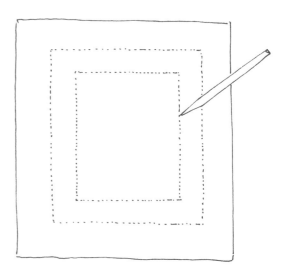

4 Using an air erasable marker, hold the fabric in front of a window or on a light table and lightly mark the outline of the interfacing on the front of the fabric. This facilitates the placement of the crochet frame that was assembled in step 2.

5 Transfer the crochet piece onto the front of the silk dupioni, and arrange the motifs until they are evenly spaced.

6 Using the fabric glue stick, place a small dab of glue on the backside of each motif by folding back the upper portion of the motif and pressing the glued motif back onto the silk.

7 Thread the #10 tapestry beading needle with doubled sewing machine thread. Start with a 5-Petal motif and couch down each side and end of each petal.

When all petals are couched in place, sew a teardrop pearl bead to the center of each petal. Pick up the teardrop pearl bead, starting at the narrow end and coming out the wider end. Stitch to the petal so that the narrow part of the bead is closest to the center.

8 Couch down the beaded connection, skipping every other bead.

9 Couch down the 3-petal motif at each side and end of each petal, bringing the needle to the front of the fabric in the center of the 3-petal loop opening. Pick up a 3mm pearl, and take the needle to the back of the fabric.

10 Repeat steps #7–9 until all the crocheted sections are stitched to the silk fabric.

Attaching the silk to the frame

1 Cut out three layers of quilt batting, slightly smaller than the front surface of the frame. Using the spray adhesive, individually glue each piece of quilt batt to the frame.

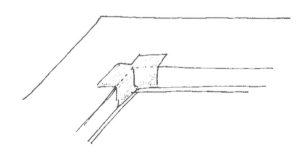

2 Cut four small pieces of silk. Apply them with spray adhesive into each corner of the interior of the frame surface. This will help camouflage the corners when the fabric covering is glued into place.

3 With the right side of the silk face down, place the frame with the quilt batting directly over the interfacing on the silk.

4 Carefully turn over the unit while holding the silk in place to double check the placement of the design on the frame surface.

5 Lightly spray the spray adhesive on the back of the frame, and wrap the silk around the outside edge of the frame, as if it were a package. Miter each corner. The silk may not stick to itself with the spray adhesive, so use the glue stick where fabric touches the frame.

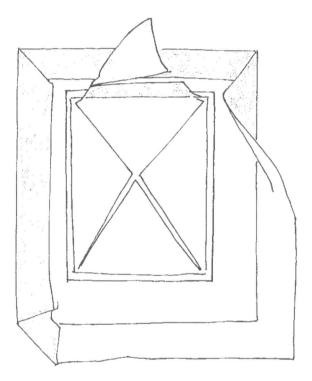

6 Slash the center of the fabric opening with a pair of scissors. Cut diagonally to each corner of the frame, stopping within ⅛" of the actual corner of the frame.

7 Apply fabric glue onto the interior surface frame, and fold the fabric of one of the inner sides to the back of the frame. Be careful not to rip the corners. Repeat with the three other sides. Make sure that the inner corners are well adhered to the frame.

8 Secure your mirror or picture into the frame, and cover the back of the frame with felt or Ultrasuede.

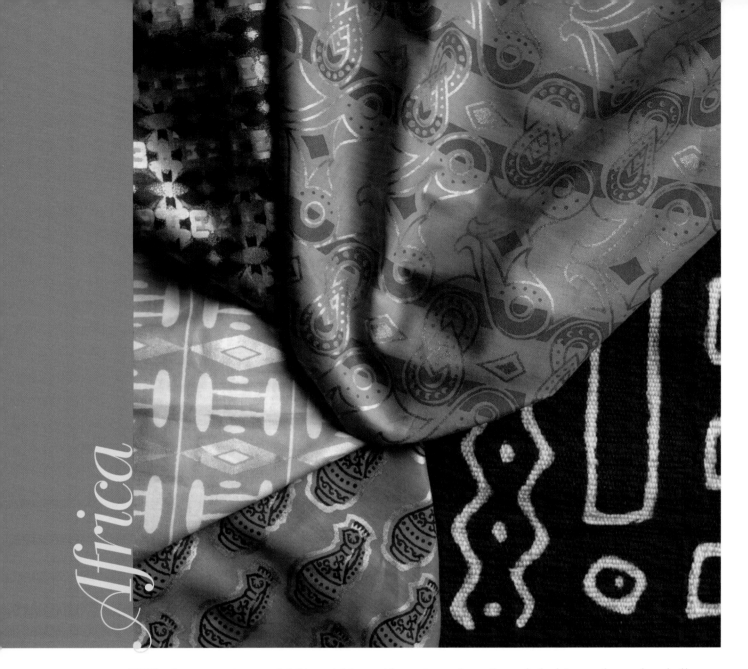

Africa

The large continent of Africa yields a wide variety of textile and clothing styles and embellishments. Textiles have bold, brightly colored geometric and abstract designs. Northern Africa is home to the Berbers. In the seventh century, the Arabs conquered these indigenous people. Their costume, the haik, descends from the Roman Toga. Necklaces with metallic discs and coins are worn with a headwrap decorated with pearls and coral. Both are symbols of fertility and are thought to ward off the evil eye.

Women in East Africa wear stunning halo-shaped necklaces of tiny beads. Animal hides are used as skirts. Cowrie shells and beads decorate leather quivers, belts, and aprons. In West Africa, women wear wrap skirts, loose fitting blouses, and a headwrap. Many types of textiles are woven, including narrow woven strips sewn together in various patterns, batik and dye methods, hand stamped adinkra cloth, and kente cloth, with the best grade of cloth reserved for kings. Men do a great deal of the embroidery in the west. The intertwined knot is a common embroidery motif. Since the introduction of beads by the Portuguese in the sixteenth century, South Africa has been known for its beadwork. Women wear lavishly beaded aprons, headbands, and necklaces. Zulu women wear high flared hats stained red with ochre.

This woman's ceremonial beaded necklace from Kenya comes from the collection of Rolf Hagberg.

The Kuba Cloth Pillow from Africa is shown on Mud Cloth from Mali.

World of Embellishment

Kuba Cloth Pillow

Supplies:

- ⅛ yd. butterscotch-colored cotton fabric
- ⅛ yd. brown cotton fabric
- ½ yd. animal print fabric
- ½ yd. fusible interfacing
- 16" pillow form
- Matching sewing thread

The Kuba people in the Democratic Republic of Congo (formally Zaire) make textiles from raffia cloth. This cloth is made from the grassy fiber of palm tree leaves. Patchwork dancing skirts were made from long lengths of raffia cloth. The skirts were decorated with appliquéd abstract designs. The most common shape is the comma-shape, known as "tail-of-the-dog."

This pillow cover uses patchwork in butterscotch and brown, typical of the raffia cloth of the Kuba. The lighter patches are decorated with two appliquéd comma-shapes, while the darker patches have two diamond shapes. The one in the background is an animal print fabric, which is also used for the back of the pillow.

All seam allowances are ½", unless noted otherwise.

1 Cut a 17" square from the animal print fabric for the back of the pillow, and cut a 17" square of interfacing. Set aside. Cut three 6½" x 9" rectangles from butterscotch-colored fabric and three from brown fabric.

2 With right sides together, sew a brown rectangle to a butterscotch rectangle along the 9" sides. On the other 9" side of the butterscotch rectangle, stitch a brown rectangle with right sides together. Sew the remaining rectangles together, with the butterscotch rectangles on either side of the remaining brown rectangle. Press all the seam allowances open.

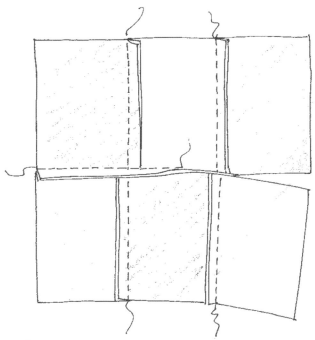

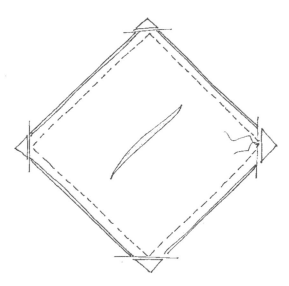

3 With right sides together, sew the strips together along the 17" sides to create a square of six patches that alternate in color. Press the seam allowances open.

4 Trace the comma-shape and both diamond pattern pieces onto lightweight cardboard to use as a template. Trace around the comma-shape onto the brown fabric and cut out. Cut 5 more comma shapes. Trace the diamond, with the center removed, onto butterscotch fabric and cut out. Cut out two more. Trace the solid diamond onto the animal print fabric and cut out. Cut out two more.

6 Place the right sides of the animal print fabric diamonds to the wrong side of the fusible interfacing. Stitch 1/4" from the edges around all sides. Clip the corners and slash the interfacing at the center of the diamond. Turn to the right side.

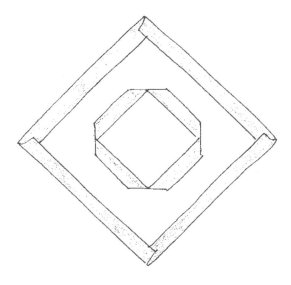

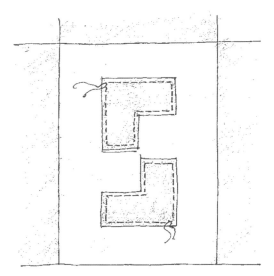

5 Press all the edges of the comma shapes ¼" to the wrong side. Place two of them in the center of a butterscotch rectangle, using the illustration as a guide. Straight stitch with contrasting thread around the shapes a scant ⅛" from the edge. Repeat with the other two butterscotch rectangles.

7 Press all the edges of the butterscotch diamonds ¼" to the wrong side, clipping the corners of the inner squares.

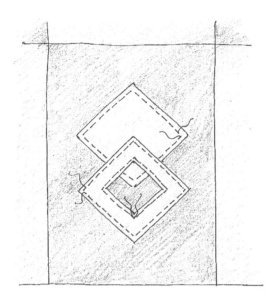

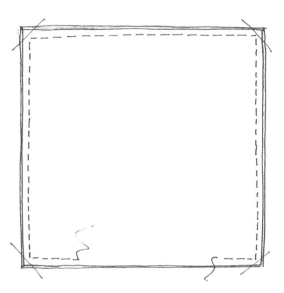

8 Using the illustration as a guide, place a solid diamond on a brown rectangle, slightly above the center of the rectangle. Press to adhere to the rectangle. Place a butterscotch diamond on top of the solid diamond so that it overlaps the lower point. Straight stitch with contrasting thread around the diamonds a scant 1/8" from the edge.

9 Fuse the interfacing to the wrong side of the pillow front. Stitch the pillow front and back with right sides together, leaving approximately 10" open along the bottom edge. Clip the corners and turn to the right side. Put the pillow form inside the pillow. Turn the unstitched seam allowances to the wrong side and slip-stitch closed.

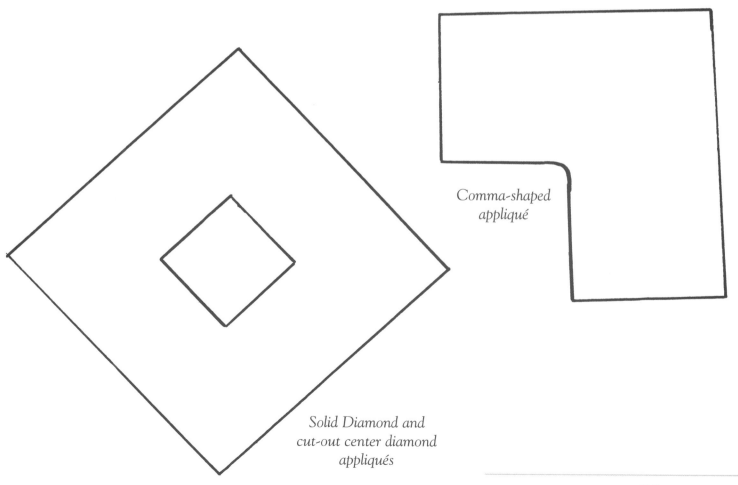

Comma-shaped appliqué

Solid Diamond and cut-out center diamond appliqués

The Ottoman Empire in the seventeenth century covered North Africa, Eastern Europe, the Middle East, and the Balkans. Its influence in textiles and clothing embellishment was far reaching. Embroidery was very important to the culture. Textiles with lavish embroidery were used as wall coverings, covers, clothing, and cushions. Clothing was flowing and loose to protect oneself from the sun and sand, but sashes, scarves, and slippers were among the embroidered items. The Arab word for embroidery is *mugassab*, which spawned the term "gussied-up."

Undyed linen was the most popular fabric used for embroidery. Two types of embroidery developed. Hesap isi is a counted thread technique. It was used on the bulk of embroidered textiles. Dival embroidery is the major style. Metallic threads are couched with cotton thread onto fabric. Metal wire spirals and sequins were added to complement the design. One characteristic of the embroidery is to frame each design with a border.

A colorfully embroidered cloth from Uzbekistan with stylized floral motifs.

Goldwork Necklace

Supplies:

- 10" square of cranberry velveteen
- 4" square of lightweight batting
- Sewing thread to match the velveteen
- 1 yd. gold cord, ⅛"
- 2" of bright check purl
- 6" of narrow bright check purl
- 10" of smooth purl
- 10" of pearl purl
- 56 gold beads, 2mm
- 5 gold beads, 3mm
- 1 small paillette or sequin
- Gold thread
- 4" square of medium weight cardboard
- 5" or 6" hoop
- Tissue or tracing paper

Motifs from the Ottoman Empire were often stylized flowers, such as tulips, hyacinths, and carnations. These designs were placed inside medallion or shield-shaped backgrounds, such as the form for this cranberry velveteen goldwork necklace.

Metal threads are available today to create the brilliant embroidery done for centuries. Purl is a long tightly-coiled round wire that can be cut into sections, threaded onto a needle, and stitched into place. Bright check purl is a wire coiled on a three-cornered needle to create an angular appearance. Pearl purl is a long coil with a "bead-like" or pearl appearance. A paillette, also known as a spangle, resembles a sequin.

The embroidery techniques using the gold purl often involve padding with a felt fabric under the floral motifs to help reflect the light from the metal coils. I have eliminated this extra step, so you will see some of the velveteen fabric showing through the petals of the flower. I designed the project to be sewn into a necklace, but it could be made into a needle case, if desired.

1 Trace the outer shape onto the velveteen with chalk. Trace the embroidery design onto the tissue paper and pin to the velveteen where marked on the pattern piece. With contrasting needle and thread, baste the outline of the design through the tissue paper and the fabric. Tear off the tissue paper.

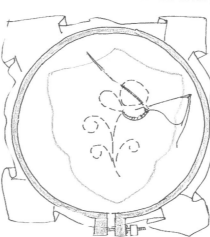

2 Put the fabric into a 5" or 6" hoop. Begin with the petals of the flower. Cut a section of pearl purl to fit around one of the petals. Bend the purl to cover the shape, being careful not to stretch the purl, and couch down with the gold thread. Repeat with the other petals. (The paillette will cover the center of the flower where the cut ends meet.)

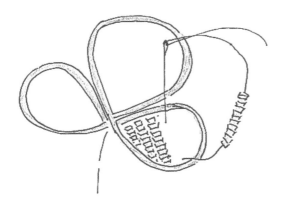

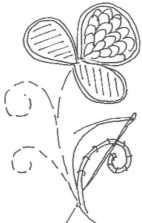

5 Cut lengths of pearl purl to cover the stems of the design. Curve each piece to fit the curve of each stem, being careful not to stretch the purl, and couch down with gold thread.

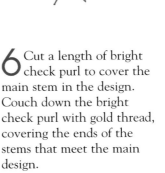

3 Cut a section of the narrow bright check purl to fit across the petal. Bring the needle with the gold thread up just inside the petal shape. Insert the needle inside the check purl and down through the fabric just inside the petal on the other side. Fill the shape with pieces of narrow bright check purl. Repeat with the other side. Keep the check purls angled in the same direction as shown in the illustration.

6 Cut a length of bright check purl to cover the main stem in the design. Couch down the bright check purl with gold thread, covering the ends of the stems that meet the main design.

7 Stitch the paillette and one of the 3mm beads to the center of the three petals.

8 Cut out the necklace, following the outline. Cut out a back necklace from the remaining fabric. Cut out the cardboard and batting, following the cardboard necklace pattern piece.

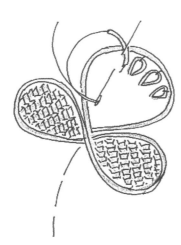

4 Cut approximately 20 sections of smooth purl, ½" in length. Bring the threaded needle up through the fabric at one of the sides at the top of the middle petal. Insert the needle through one of the smooth purl sections and go back down through the fabric next to the first thread. This will create a loop. Take a stitch at the top of the loop to secure it to the fabric. Fill the top of the petal with loops, keeping them inside the pearl purl outline. Make another row slightly below the first row. Make two to three more rows to fill in the shape.

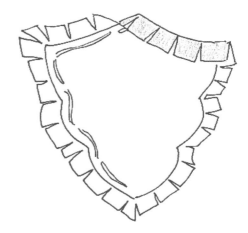

9 Place the cardboard necklace on the wrong side of the necklace back. Slash the curves of the seam allowance of the necklace back and fold the fabric over the cardboard, gluing in place.

10 Glue the batting to the other side of the cardboard. Place the necklace front over the batting and cardboard, clipping the curves and turning the seam allowance under. With matching thread, stitch the front to the back around the edge.

11 Cut the gold cord to fit around the outside of the necklace. Stitch it to the necklace edge, hiding the ends at the back. Stitch each end of the remaining cord to each side of the top of the necklace, slipping the ends between the front and the back.

12 Cut a length of thread, and string 11 of the 3mm beads and then a 4mm bead. Go back through all of the 3mm beads to the top. Make four more strings of beads and attach them all at the same spot on the point of the necklace.

Template for cardboard

Template for embroidery design

Outer shape cutting line for front and back

Mary Beth Tarnowski wears the Vest with Gold Trim.

Vest with Gold Trim

Supplies:

- Vest pattern with round neckline*
- Navy velveteen for the vest
- Navy fabric for the lining
- 18" wide x 10" long burgundy velveteen
- Clear invisible thread
- For size X-large:
  8¼ yd. gold braided trim, ¼" wide
  5¾ yd. flexible gold trim, ⅛" wide
  2 yd. gold trim, ½" wide
  1½ yd. flexible gold cord, ⅛" wide
- Water-soluble glue stick
- Tissue or tracing paper

*I used Paw Prints Versatile Vest.

Loose-fitting vests with high round necklines are worn in many areas from Greece to Pakistan. They are usually dark in color with gold braids stitched around the edges in a variety of patterns. The technique for attaching the braids or cords is called couching. A matching thread is stitched over the cords or braids at intervals. The majestic look of these couched metal threads has been used on clerical robes and military uniforms throughout the world.

The vest shown here is a basic style. The braids are zigzag stitched in place with clear invisible thread, instead of being couched by hand. The burgundy patches with the tiny gold braid, typical of the appliqués seen on vests from Pakistan, add interest to the garment.

1 Cut out the fronts and back of the vest. Stitch the fronts and back at the shoulder seams with right sides together. Press the seams open.

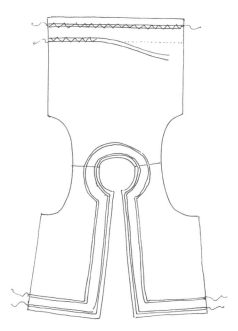

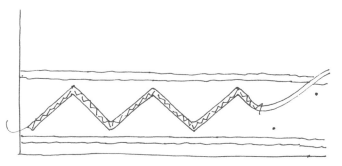

5 Begin marking along the inside row of braid, marking directly across from the mark along the outside row. Make a mark 1" away from the first one. Continue measuring and marking every 2" on the neckline, stopping at the corner. Continue marking every 2", as in step #4. Repeat with the other side.

2 Beginning at the lower front edge, stitch the ¼" gold braid to the vest ¾" away from the edge with a zigzag stitch and clear invisible thread. Stitch along the lower edge, up one of the center fronts, around the neckline, down the other center front and along the other lower front edge. Stitch along the lower back edge also.

3 Measure 2" in from the braid and draw a line with chalk. Stitch another row of the ¼" gold braid over this line, as in step #2, on the neckline, center fronts, and the lower front and back edges.

6 Pin the ⅛" gold trim on the neckline at the first mark along the outside row of braid. Stitch the gold trim with a zigzag stitch and clear invisible thread, using a braiding presser foot if you have one. Stitch from the first mark to the next one along the inside row of braid and then back to the next mark along the outside row. You will create a zigzag pattern with the gold trim. When you reach a corner, make a loop (see photo) and continue with the zigzag pattern. Make a loop at the lower front corner and continue stitching the trim in the same zigzag pattern until you reach the side seam. Repeat with the other side.

7 Make the same marks between the braids along the lower back edge of vest and stitch the trim, using the same zigzag pattern.

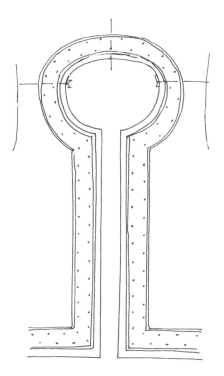

4 Beginning at the center of the back neckline, make a mark with chalk next to the first row of braid. Measure 2" away and make another mark. Make marks every 2" until you reach the front corner. Leave this area open. Continue marking every 2" down the vest until you reach the lower corner. Leave this area open and continue marking every 2" on the lower front. Repeat with the other side.

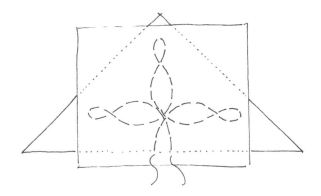

8 Use the pattern piece to cut out four triangles from the burgundy velveteen. Trace the design shown on the pattern piece onto tissue paper. Place the tissue paper with the design on the velveteen triangle where shown on the pattern piece. With needle and thread, baste along the lines to mark the design on the fabric. Tear away the paper.

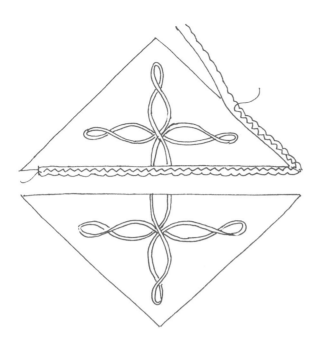

10 Place two of the triangles on one of the lower fronts, as shown in the photo. Stitch the ½" trim to the edges of each triangle, turning the end under when you have finished stitching. Repeat with the remaining triangles on the other lower front.

11 Sew the ¼" gold braid to the armholes, stitching with a zigzag stitch and clear invisible thread. The trim should be placed ¾" from the cut edges.

12 Construct the vest with the lining, following the pattern instructions.

Close-up of the trim on the velveteen appliqúes.

9 Using the glue stick, glue the ⅛" cord to the design. Stitch the design with a narrow zigzag stitch and clear invisible thread. Repeat with all four of the triangles.

Triangle pattern piece

India has a rich history in embroidered textiles. As early as 300 B.C., wealthy citizens wore embroidered clothing. Marco Polo visited this sub-continent on his way back from China and noted the high quality of embroideries. Because the country was positioned along the old trade routes to Asia, it had many influences throughout history. Textiles came from China along the Silk Road. Western countries, such as Holland, Britain, and Portugal were able to land on India's vast coastline to establish trade.

The most well known clothing style for women is the sari, which has drapes and folds from many yards of fabric. Another clothing style for women is the salwar-kameez, a long tunic worn with baggy pants that are fitted at the ankle. Men wear a type of loincloth that resembles draped trousers called dhoti.

The vast embellishment techniques for clothing and textiles are made with a variety of materials. Applique, whitework, counted thread work, pattern darning, and quilting are just a few examples. The stitching is done with cotton and silk thread. Shisha, or mirror work, attaches tiny mirrors to fabric with thread. Gold and silver threads have been embroidered on a variety of grounds, including silk and velvet. Metallic green beetle wings have been used as a form of sequins. Other materials include beads imported from Europe, cowrie shells, coins, buttons, and tassels.

Opposite page: A tunic from India that has Shisha mirror embroidery. This page: Shanti Lakhan has a collection of costumes from India and Pakistan. She wears her latest purchase, a salwar-kameez from Islamabad. It is embroidered with beads in small floral designs.

Placemat and Napkin with Shisha Embroidery

Supplies:

- Purchased sheer gold fabric placemat and napkin
- Small square red satin fabric
- Red and green heavyweight rayon decorative thread
- Purple metallic machine embroidery thread
- Green machine embroidery thread
- Green and purple embroidery floss
- 5 round mirrors, ¾"
- Water-soluble stabilizer

Mirrors have always had special significance around the world. With their reflective qualities, they have been thought to deflect evil by holding the attention of the evil eye. Mirrors have a connection to magic by the way they capture the sunlight and return it. *Shisha*, or mirror work, has been credited to the wife of Shah Jahan, whose husband built the Taj Mahal in her honor. The mirrors have no holes so they are applied to fabric with surrounding threads in a variety of stitches. Embroidered mirrors are thought to have protective qualities for the wearer of the garment.

This placemat and napkin have mirrors stitched to a red satin square appliqué, which is typical of Indian embroidery. The mirrors are attached with rows of buttonhole stitches that extend over the surface of the mirrors to secure them. You can use other items instead of mirrors, such as large sequins. The purchased placemat and napkin are made of a gold metallic fabric, which complements the Shisha embroidery, but any fabric can be used.

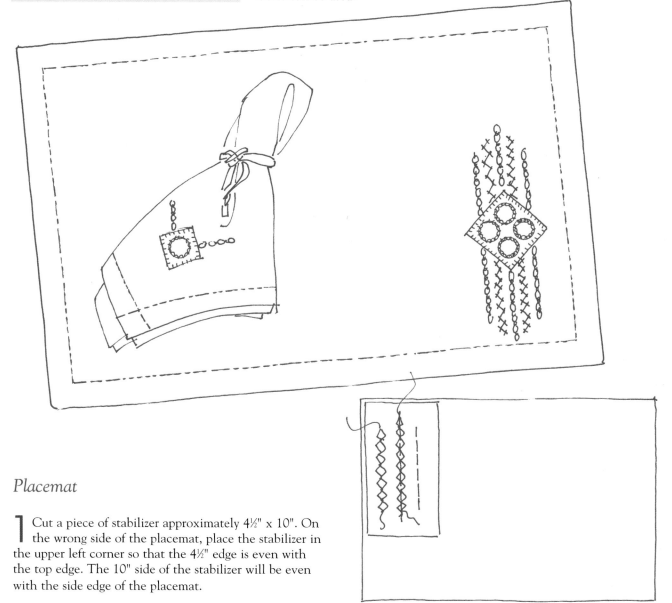

Placemat

1 Cut a piece of stabilizer approximately 4½" x 10". On the wrong side of the placemat, place the stabilizer in the upper left corner so that the 4½" edge is even with the top edge. The 10" side of the stabilizer will be even with the side edge of the placemat.

2 Measure 1" from the top and 2½" from the side edge, and draw an 8" line vertically on the stabilizer. Thread red sewing thread in the needle and fill a bobbin with the red heavyweight thread. Place the bobbin in the machine, but do not put the thread in the tension. Place the side with the stabilizer under the needle, and stitch a row of decorative stitches such as diamonds on the drawn line. The heavier bobbin thread will curl on the right side of the placemat.

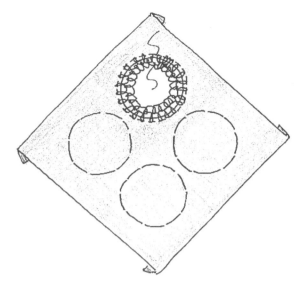

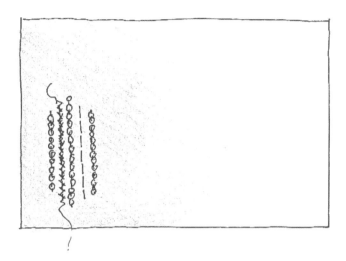

3 Measure ¾" to the right of the red stitching. Draw a 7" line beginning 1½" from the top of the placemat. Repeat on the left side of the red stitching. Thread green sewing thread in the needle and green heavyweight thread in the bobbin. Stitch rows of green diamonds as in step #2.

4 Turn the placemat to the right side. With washout marker, beginning 1¼" from the top edge, draw a 7⅜" line centered between the red and green stitching. Repeat in between the red and green stitching on the other side. Thread the purple metallic thread in the needle and purple sewing thread in the bobbin. (Be sure the bobbin thread is placed in the tension.) Stitch rows of decorative stitches such as herringbone stitches over the drawn lines.

5 Remove the stabilizer with water.

6 Cut a square of red satin, using the pattern piece for the placemat. Press all edges under ¼".

7 Trace each of the mirrors on the red fabric where marked on the pattern piece. With a long strand of green embroidery floss (use all six strands) work backstitches (⅛" long) around one of the circles. Do not tie off. Place the mirror on the circle, and begin working a buttonhole stitch, catching each of the backstitches. Continue making a second row of buttonhole stitches in each of the loops of the first row. At the end of the second row, check to see if the mirror is held securely. Some thicker mirrors may require a third row. Bring the thread to the wrong side of the fabric and tie off. Stitch another mirror with green floss in the opposite corner. Stitch the remaining two mirrors to the fabric with the purple floss.

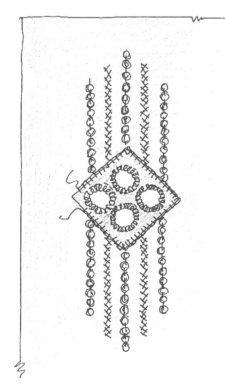

8 Place the mirror embroidery on the placemat, centering it over the decoratively stitched lines. With green machine embroidery thread, attach it to the placemat using machine or hand-worked blanket stitches.

Napkin

1 Cut a 5½" square of water-soluble stabilizer, and place it on the wrong side of one corner of the napkin. The edges should be flush with the sides of the napkin. Mark a point 2½" from each side. Draw a line from this point extending 2" in each direction, creating a right angle.

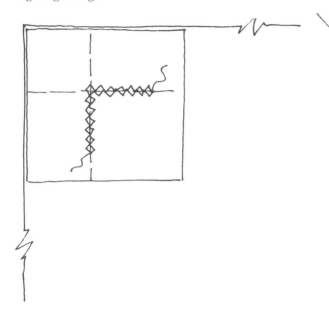

2 Following step #2 of the Placemat instructions, stitch decorative stitches with the heavyweight green thread in the bobbin. Remove the stabilizer with water.

3 Cut a square of red satin using the pattern piece for the napkin. Press all edges under ¼".

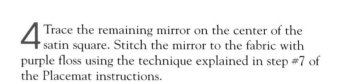

4 Trace the remaining mirror on the center of the satin square. Stitch the mirror to the fabric with purple floss using the technique explained in step #7 of the Placemat instructions.

5 Center the embroidered square over the corner of the decorative stitches. Attach the fabric to the placemat with green machine embroidery thread using machine or hand-worked blanket stitches.

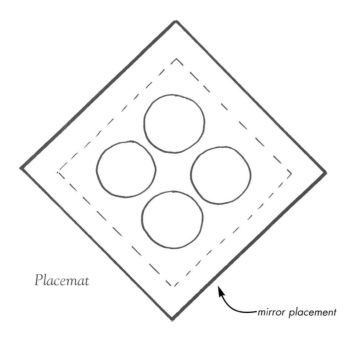

Placemat

mirror placement

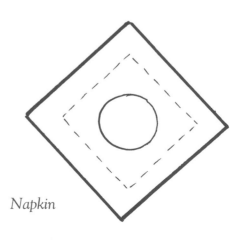

Napkin

Beaded Tunic

Supplies:

- Pattern for a sleeveless tunic with a front opening*
- Brocade fabric for the tunic
- Lining fabric for the tunic
- ½ yd. each silk dupioni fabric in three colors, matching the brocade
- 1 hank size 11 seed beads in one of the silk fabric colors
- 1 hank bugle beads to match seed beads, 4mm
- 66 gold bugle beads, 4mm
- 6 size 6 gold beads
- Nymo beading thread
- #10 tapestry beading needle
- Clear invisible thread
- 8 hook-and-eye closures

*I used Butterick #3249.

The teardrop motif, known as the paisley, has been used in India for centuries, but it gets its name from a Scottish village. The motif developed from a stylized mango and was incorporated into many textiles across India. Originating from a single flower with leaves, it was known as the "princely-flower" in Persia. Eventually the motif developed its elongated cone shape, but its tip could bend to the right or left. In the Victorian era, shawls from Kashmir that used this motif became very popular in Europe. Factories across Europe sprang up, producing less costly imitations. Paisley, Scotland produced some of the highest quality shawls.

This sleeveless beaded tunic is my version of the *salwar-kameez*. It's made from a shiny brocade fabric with a beaded panel along each side of the center front opening, making it ideal for eveningwear. The panel has six hand-beaded paisley motifs. If you have access to an embroidery machine with paisley motifs, you may prefer to stitch them on the front instead. Capri pants, popular today, complete the ensemble.

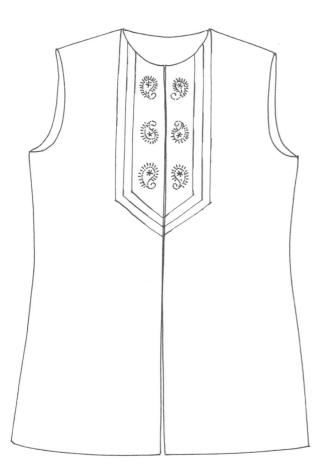

1 Cut out two fronts and one back from the brocade and the lining fabric.

2 For the panels in the front, cut two rectangles 3¼" x 13" from one of the colors of silk. Measure 3¼" from one of the ends and draw a line to the other corner to create a 45 degree angle. Cut along this line. Repeat with the other rectangle.

3 Cut two rectangles 3¾" x 13½" from one of the other colors of silk fabric. Cut a 45 degree angle along one of the ends as in step #2. Cut two rectangles 4¼" x 14" from the remaining color of silk fabric. Cut a 45 degree angle along one of the ends as above.

4 Press the short side and the diagonal end of one of the 13" pieces ½" to the wrong side. (Use a piece of cardboard to fold the edges over. This will keep the folds straight.) Repeat with the other side. Be sure that the pieces are mirror images of each other. Press the short side and diagonal end of the remaining pieces ½" to the wrong side.

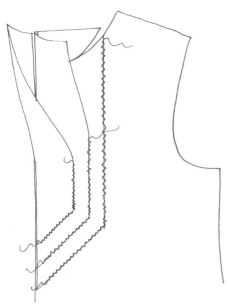

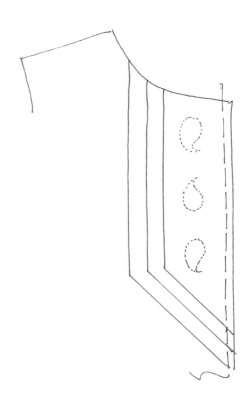

5 Pin one of the 14" long pieces on the top of the center front opening of the tunic so that the edges are flush. Trim any excess extending at the neck along the neckline curve. Using the clear invisible thread, sew along the folded edges with a very narrow zigzag stitch. Pin one of the 13½" pieces on top of the first one so that the cut edge is flush with the tunic center front edge. The bottom piece should extend about ½" beyond the top one. Stitch with a very narrow zigzag stitch. Place the remaining 13" piece on top of the others as above. Stitch along the folded edges as above. Repeat with the other side of the tunic.

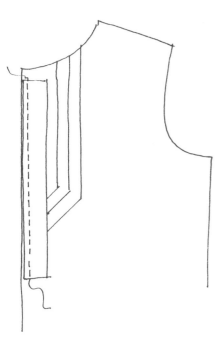

6 Measure from the neckline to the waist on the left front tunic. Cut a flap to fit under the placket 3" wide and this measurement long. Fold this flap in half lengthwise with right sides together, and stitch across each end with a ½" seam allowance. Turn to the right side and press. Pin the flap along the left front opening. The top edge should be placed ¾" below the cut edge of the neckline. Stitch the flap to the center front of the tunic ½" from the cut edges.

7 Baste along the cut edges of the right tunic front. Measure ½" from the front cut edges, and draw a line with a chalk pencil. This will be the right front seam line. Trace around the paisley pattern piece and cut one from cardboard or plastic. Place the paisley on one of the front edges 1¼" from the top edge, centering it between the drawn line and the stitched edge of the silk fabric. Trace around it with a chalk pencil. Extending the line at the point of the paisley, draw the curved spiral as shown in the illustration. Trace two more paisleys on the front edge so that they are evenly spaced. The center paisley should be turned upside down.

8 For the left side of the tunic, press the flap/tunic seam towards the tunic. Trace the paisleys on the fabric as in Step #7, using the pressed seam as a guide instead of the chalk line.

Paisley template

*Beaded template
with swirl*

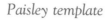

9 Thread one of the needles with a long length of thread, and knot. Come from the back of the fabric at the edge of the paisley outline. Put three of the size 11 seed beads on the needle, and go back through the fabric very close to the bead on the design line. Come back up between the first and second beads and go through between beads two and three again. Pick up three more beads and repeat the procedure until the outline is completed. (This is called the beaded backstitch.)

10 Stitch the matching bugle beads perpendicular to the outline of the paisley, spacing them a scant ¼" apart.

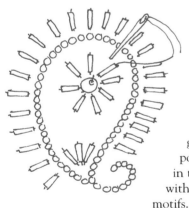

11 Measure ½" from the rounded edge of the paisley towards the center. Sew a size 6 bead at this spot. Sew eight gold bugle beads around the size 6 bead in a radiating pattern. Sew three gold bugle beads inside the point of the paisley as shown in the illustration. Repeat with the remaining paisley motifs.

12 Construct the remainder of the tunic, following the pattern instructions. Sew the tunic to the lining using the drawn line at the right front and the flap/tunic seam on the left front as the seam lines.

13 Sew the hook side of the hook-and-eye closure under the right front at the neckline. Sew the eye to the flap on the left side at the neckline. Sew the remaining evenly spaced hooks and eyes to the front opening.

Close-up of beaded paisleys.

Far East

China was the first civilization to learn to spin and weave cloth from silk. Silk and metal thread stitching on silk fabric is characteristic of Chinese embroideries. Satin stitch and the Peking knot, or forbidden knot, are common embroidery techniques. The design motifs have symbolic significance. Flowers such as the peony, iris, and chrysanthemum all signify feminine attributes. The phoenix, usually reserved for the empress, stands for beauty and good fortune. Basic traditional dress consists of a hip-length tunic with a diagonal front opening worn over loose trousers.

Wearing kimono dress in Japan is an art form. The crossover open robe maintains a simple silhouette, creating an emphasis on rich fabrics and beautiful embroidery. Imperial court dress was decorated with embroidery in silk and metal threads, painting, and tie-dyeing. The kimono is worn today for formal occasions, such as weddings and classes in traditional arts. Western designers have embraced the kimono because it does not reveal the figure. It can be worn by both sexes, and it appears ageless. Japan's textile manufacturing techniques, such as indigo-dyeing, are revered by its citizens.

This Chinese robe from the 1920s is embroidered with silk using primarily satin stitches and floral and dragon motifs.

Chinese Brocade Shirt
with Custom Clothes Fasteners

Supplies:

- Pattern for shirt that has a mandarin collar, short sleeves, and a side closure*
- Silk or silk blend brocade fabric
- Solid color fabric to match silk brocade for piping
- Cording, ¼" wide, to go around the top of the collar and side closure
- 1 skein #5 perle cotton to match the solid color fabric
- Hand mixer with one beater

*I used Simplicity #9868.

Western influence was adopted in China with the formation of the Republic in 1912. The Chinese robe, or *ao*, became slimmer and longer with narrower sleeves. It was worn over an ankle-length skirt. By 1925, the top and skirt became a one-piece garment called a *qi pao*. In the 1940s, the *qi pao* was a slim-fitting, short- or cap-sleeved dress. The standup collar was piped on both sides, and frog buttons were placed at the diagonal front closure.

The style of the *qi pao* is still fashionable today. Patterns can be found for a dress or shirt with a collar and diagonal closure. I chose to make this style of shirt from a Chinese silk brocade fabric. The beautiful butterfly print in two shades of pink does not require further embellishment. The front opening has custom frog closures made from a handmade twisted cord. You will be able to make a match with any fabric color if you make your own twisted cord, giving your clothing a couture touch.

1 Cut a 1½" bias strip from the solid color fabric as long as the cording. Wrap the wrong side of the fabric around the cording and stitch close to the cording. Trim the seam allowance to ½". Assemble the shirt according to the pattern instructions, sewing the piping to the top edge of the right side of the collar and around the neckline and front closure.

2 For the closures, make a twisted cord from the perle cotton. Cut two 10-yard lengths of perle cotton. Fold each one in half, and slide a pencil in the fold. Tie the cut ends to the end of a beater from a hand mixer. Have a friend hold the pencil with the folded cord while you hold the mixer. The perle cotton should be held taut. Turn the mixer on medium speed to twist the perle cotton tightly. Walk towards each other, folding the perle cotton in the middle, and the perle cotton will twist back on itself to form a cord. Cut the cord off the mixer and tie a knot to prevent untwisting. You should have approximately two yards of cord.

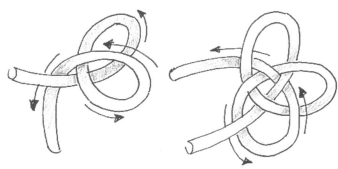

5 Make the knotted end of the closure. Make a Chinese button knot in the center of the 14½" cord, following the illustrations. Measure 1" from the ball on each side of the cord, and stitch together with perle cotton. Roll each end into a tight circle as in step #4, stopping when you reach the knotted center. Repeat with the other side. Make two more knotted closures.

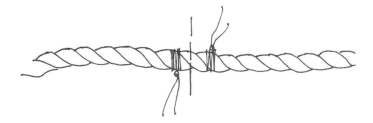

3 For the three loop ends of the closures, measure 13½" of cord, wrap a short length of remaining perle cotton around the cord at this point, and secure. Measure another ¼" from the wrapped cord, and wrap another length of perle cotton around the cord. Now you can cut between the wrappings and they will not unravel. Repeat until you have three 13½" lengths of cord. For the knotted ends of the closures, cut three 14½" lengths of the cord, following the same procedure.

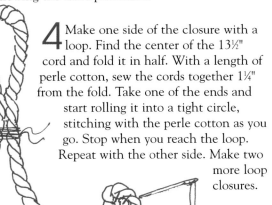

4 Make one side of the closure with a loop. Find the center of the 13½" cord and fold it in half. With a length of perle cotton, sew the cords together 1¼" from the fold. Take one of the ends and start rolling it into a tight circle, stitching with the perle cotton as you go. Stop when you reach the loop. Repeat with the other side. Make two more loop closures.

6 Mark placement of the closures on each side of the opening. Stitch the knotted side on the top part of the shirt, so that the button knot just covers the piping. The loop side is stitched on the bottom part with the loop extending slightly beyond the piping.

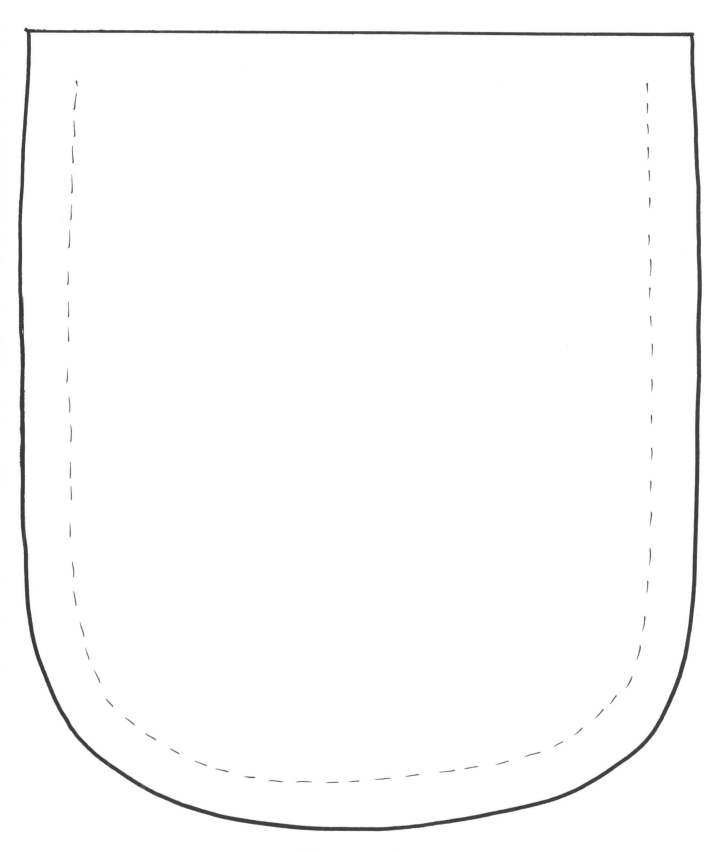

Chinese Purse front

Chinese Purse with Butterfly Knotted Closure

Supplies:

- ½ yd. silk or silk-blend brocade fabric
- ½ yd. thin batting
- 1 yd. pink fabric for lining and piping
- 38" cording, ¼" wide, for piping
- 1 yd. thick decorative cord for strap
- 1 skein fuchsia #5 perle cotton
- 2 beads with large holes
- Hand mixer with one beater

The Chinese shirt needs its own shoulder purse. The purse shape was taken from a sketch of purses in a peddler's cart in China during the 1920s. The front flap is fastened by a Chinese knotted closure shaped like butterflies. The center knot of the butterfly is a *sauvastika* knot. The *sauvastika* is the sister to the *swastika*. Both are ancient Buddhist motifs resembling Buddha's heart. Tying knots may require a little practice. Try pinning the cords to a piece of thick cardboard to hold them in place while knotting.

All seam allowances ½".

Chinese Purse

1 From the pattern pieces, cut out one purse with flap and one front purse from brocade. Cut out the same pieces from the lining and the batting.

2 Baste the batting to the wrong sides of the brocade purse pieces. Trim the batting from the seam allowances close to the stitching.

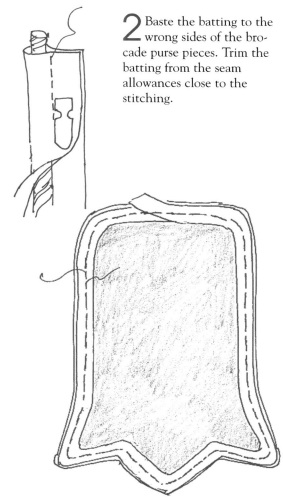

3 To make the piping, cut a 1½" bias strip from the solid color fabric as long as the cording. Wrap the wrong side of the fabric around the cording and stitch close to the cording. Trim the seam allowance to ½". Baste the piping around the brocade purse with flap, overlapping along one side.

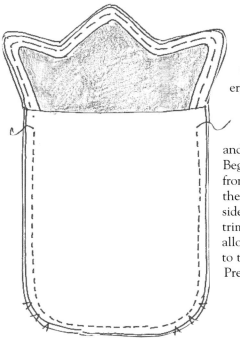

4 With right sides together, sew the front purse to the purse with flap along the sides and bottom edge. Begin stitching the front purse ½" from the top edge on each side. Clip the curves, trim the seam allowances, and turn to the right side. Press.

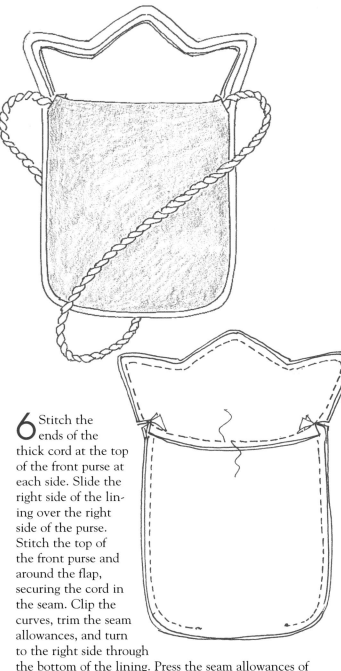

5 Sew the purse with flap lining to the front purse lining with right sides together, beginning ½" from the top side edges. Leave a four- to six-inch opening in the bottom of the lining to turn. Clip the curves, trim the seam allowances, and turn to the right side. Press.

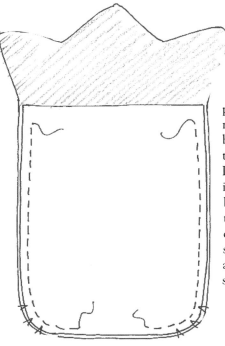

6 Stitch the ends of the thick cord at the top of the front purse at each side. Slide the right side of the lining over the right side of the purse. Stitch the top of the front purse and around the flap, securing the cord in the seam. Clip the curves, trim the seam allowances, and turn to the right side through the bottom of the lining. Press the seam allowances of the open area of the bottom of the lining to the wrong side, and slipstitch closed. Press the lining of the purse to the inside.

Butterfly Knotted Closure

1 Make a twisted cord from the perle cotton for the closures. Cut two lengths of perle cotton 8 yards long. Fold each one in half, and slide a pencil in the fold. Tie the cut ends to the end of a beater from a hand mixer. Have a friend hold the pencil with the folded cord while you hold the mixer. The perle cotton should be held taut. Turn the mixer on medium speed to twist the perle cotton tightly. Walk towards each other, folding the perle cotton in the middle, and the perle cotton will twist back on itself to form a cord. Cut the cord off the mixer and tie a knot to prevent untwisting. You should have approximately 1½ yards of cord.

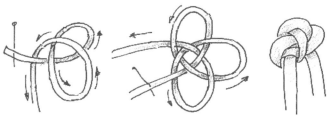

2 Folding the cord in half, wrap a short length of the remaining perle cotton around the cord at this point, and secure. Measure another ¼" from the wrapped cord and wrap another length of perle cotton around the cord. Now you can cut between the wrappings, and they will not unravel.

3 Make the loop side of the butterfly. Fold one piece of cord in half, and make a ¾" loop. Begin tying the sauvasti-ka knot, as shown in the illustrations. The loops at the sides should be approximately 1" long. Fold the remaining cords to make two more loops under the first. The remaining cords will hang below the loops. Using perle cotton, sew the loops together at the center.

4 Measure ½" down from the center on each cord and wrap with perle cotton as described in step #2. Cut the cords just beyond this point. Hide the cords under the center knot, and stitch in place.

5 Following the illustrations, make a Chinese ball knot in the center of the remaining cord. Tie the sauvasti-ka knot ½" below the ball knot, following the illustrations. Keep the loops at the sides approximately 1" long. Fold the remaining cords to make two more loops under the first. The remaining cords will hang below the loops. Using perle cotton, sew the loops together at the center.

6 Measure down the cords 1½" from the center knot. Wrap with perle cotton as described in step #2, and cut the cords just beyond this point. Slide the beads on the cords and rein-force with more stitching so that the beads will stay.

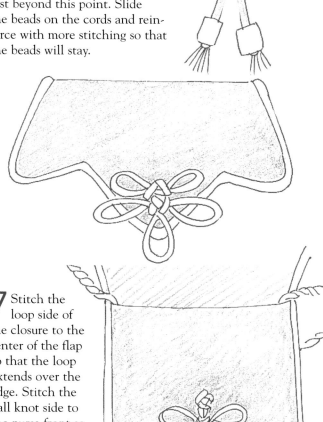

7 Stitch the loop side of the closure to the center of the flap so that the loop extends over the edge. Stitch the ball knot side to the purse front so that the ball will be caught in the loop.

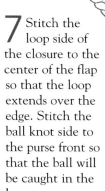

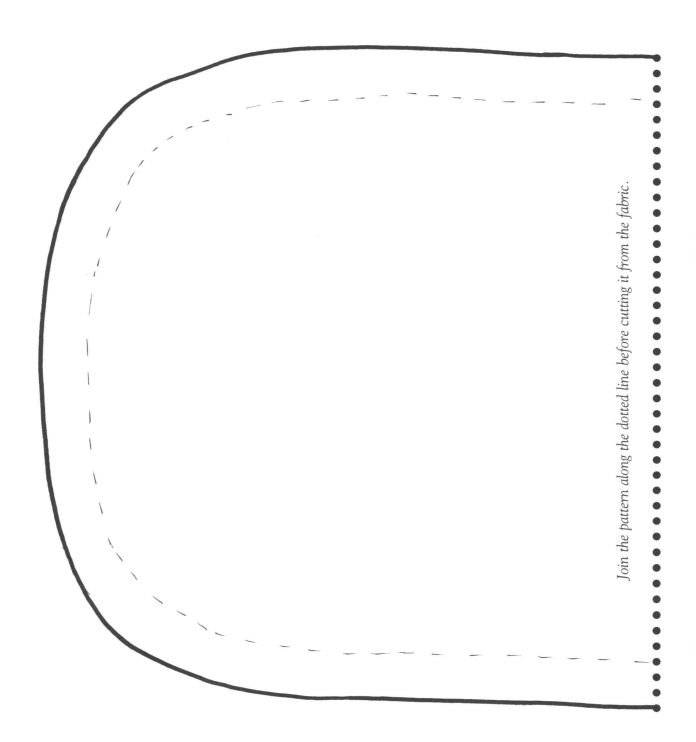

Join the pattern along the dotted line before cutting it from the fabric.

Chinese Purse with Flap

Purse front is on page 115.

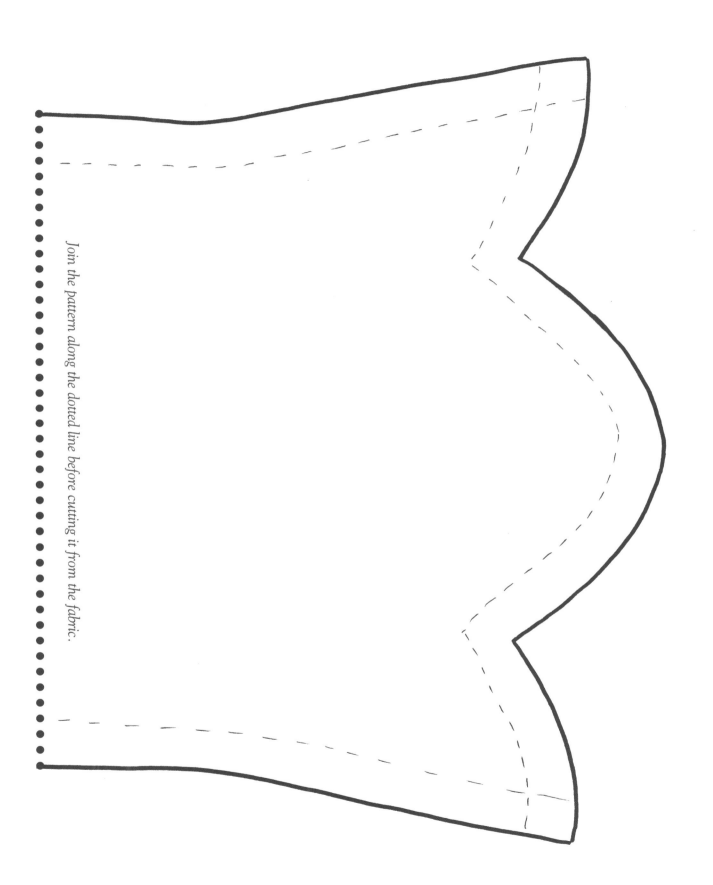

Join the pattern along the dotted line before cutting it from the fabric.

World of Embellishment

Checkbook Cover and Needle Case with Kogin Embroidery

Supplies for embroidery:
- 6" square of #22 Hardanger fabric
- 1 yd. #5 perle cotton, color #336
- 2 sets of 6" stretcher bars
- #24 tapestry needle

Supplies for checkbook cover:
- 14" x 7½" indigo print fabric
- 4" square of lightweight fusible interfacing
- Glue stick

Supplies for needle case:
- 14" x 5½" indigo print fabric
- 2½" x 4" dark blue wool felt
- 3" x 4½" dark blue Ultrasuede,
- 4" square lightweight fusible interfacing
- Glue stick

(Designed by Marilee Sagat)

The Tsugaru peninsula on Honshu Island in Japan was the birthplace of *Kogin* embroidery. While the people of this island were not permitted to purchase supplies from any other area in the 1600s, they made clothing from natural hemp and flax. Darning the indigo-dyed clothing with white cotton thread, the women achieved both reinforcement and warmth. This embroidery is a form of pattern darning, which has counted running stitches woven over and under the threads of the fabric. Most of the patterns are diamond shapes or other geometric shapes.

The "spirit" of *Kogin* embroidery is continued in this multicultural checkbook cover and needle case. They have been constructed from indigo-dyed fabric, which was imported from England, but made in South Africa. The embroidery design is the Chinese symbol for peace. No interfacing was needed, because the indigo fabric is quite stiff. The checkbook cover has pockets for the checks and the register. The needle case contains a piece of wool felt for needles and a pocket for scissors. If you choose a lighter-weight fabric, experiment with interfacing. Don't forget a beaded tassel for your scissors!

Embroidery

1 Tack the fabric to the stretcher bars.

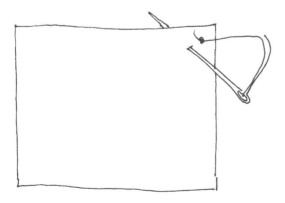

2 Thread one end of the needle, and place an away knot in the upper right hand corner of the frame, bringing the needle from the front to the back so that the knot remains on the right side of the fabric.

3 Follow the graph to stitch the embroidery design. Stitch with a running stitch, going under and over the threads marked on the graph. The rows of stitches worked back and forth. The stitches should be worked in the direction of the arrows marked on the graph.

4 When the stitching is complete, cut the away knot and weave in both the ends of the thread on the back of the design.

5 Take the fabric off the stretcher bars and press on the wrong side.

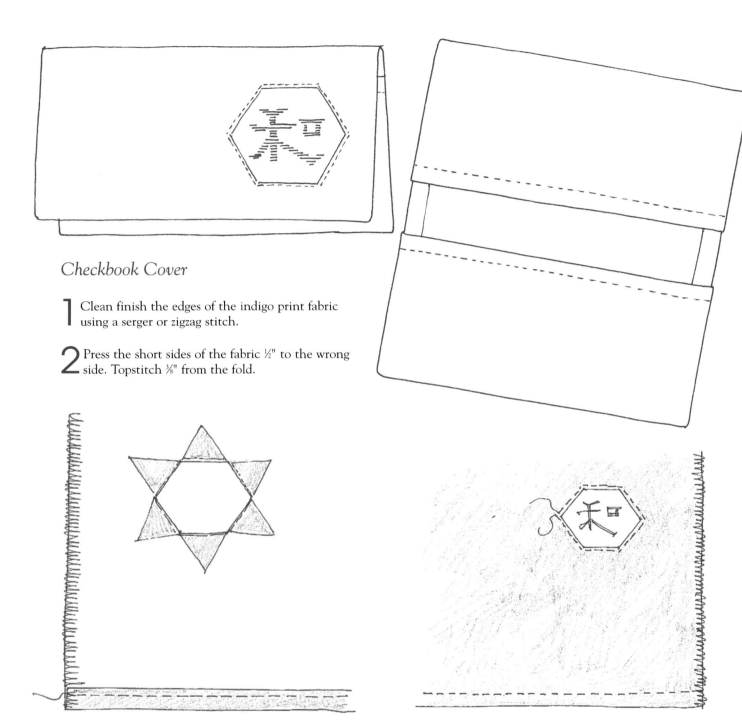

Checkbook Cover

1 Clean finish the edges of the indigo print fabric using a serger or zigzag stitch.

2 Press the short sides of the fabric ½" to the wrong side. Topstitch ⅜" from the fold.

3 Hold the fabric so that the short sides are on the top and bottom. Place the hexagon template 4" from the bottom and 1" from the right side of the long edge. Trace the shape with chalk on the fabric. Using a sewing machine, stitch on the chalk line. When the sewing is completed, slit the center of the hexagon and clip from the center to each corner. Carefully fold back the six flaps along the stitching line and press.

4 Dab each flap with the glue stick. Center the stitching in the hexagon, and lightly finger press. The glue will hold the embroidery in place for stitching. Topstitch very closely to the edge of the indigo fabric.

5 Iron a small piece of interfacing on the backside of the hexagon. Trim away all excess fabric to within ¼" of the stitching.

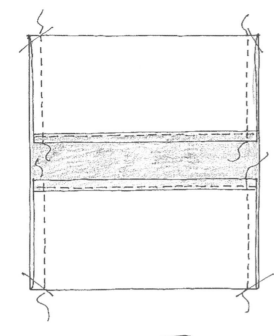

6 Fold the embroidered short side 3" towards the center with right sides together. Stitch the edges together along the long sides with a ½" seam allowance. Fold the other short side 2¾" towards the center with right sides together, and stitch these edges together with a ½" seam allowance.

7 Clip each corner and turn to the right side. Press all edges, including the section of seam allowance in the center, on each side.

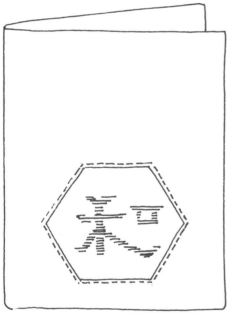

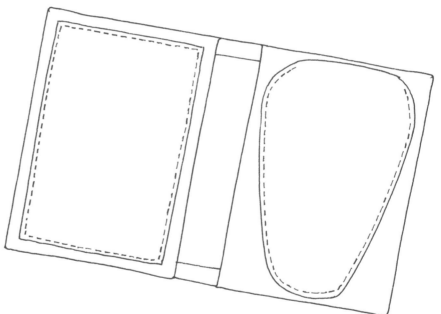

Needle Case

1 Clean finish all of the edges using a serger or zigzag stitch.

2 Press each short side of the fabric ½" to the wrong side. Topstitch ⅜" from the fold.

3 Hold the fabric with the right side up so that the long sides are on the top and bottom. Measure 3-3/8" from the right hand short side and 1" from the bottom on the long side. Trace the hexagon with the chalk on the fabric. Using a sewing machine, stitch on the chalk line. When the sewing is completed, slit the center of the hexagon and clip from the center to each corner. Carefully fold back the six flaps along the stitching line and press.

4 Dab each flap with glue stick. Center the stitching in the center of the hexagon and lightly finger press. The glue will hold the embroidery in place for stitching. Topstitch very closely to the edge of the indigo fabric.

5 Iron a small piece of interfacing on the backside of the hexagon. This protects the stitching from pulling during use of the checkbook cover. Trim away all excess fabric to within ¼" of the stitching.

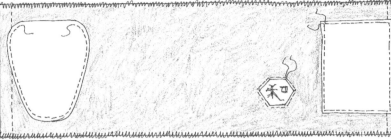

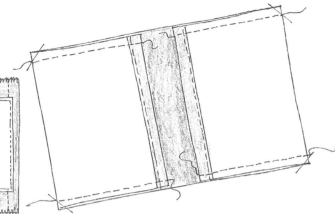

6 Pin the wool felt on the right side of the fabric ¼" from the stitched short side. Stitch close to the edge on all sides.

7 Using the scissors pocket pattern piece, cut out the pocket from Ultrasuede. Pin the pocket to the left side of the needle case ¼" from the stitched edge. Stitch it to the fabric on the lines drawn on the pattern piece, leaving an opening at the top for the scissors.

8 Fold each short side 3" towards the center with right sides together. Stitch along the long sides of the needle case with a scant ⅜" seam allowance. Clip each corner and turn right side out. Push out the corners and press.

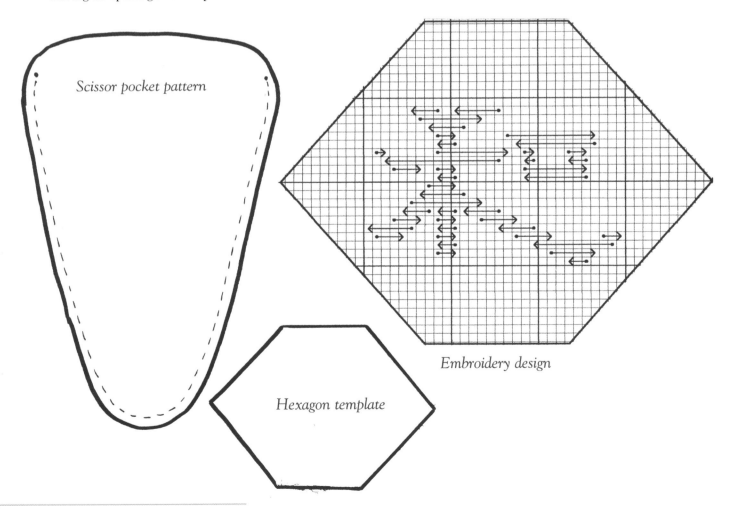

Scissor pocket pattern

Hexagon template

Embroidery design

Bibliography

General Costume and Embroidery Books

Folkwear Patterns. Asheville, NC: Earth Guild.

Gillow, John, and Bryan Sentence. *World Textiles.* London: Thames and Hudson Ltd, 1999.

Gostelow, Mary. *The Complete International Book of Embroidery.* New York: Simon and Shuster, 1977.

Kennett, Frances. *Ethnic Dress.* Great Britain: Reed International Books Limited, 1995.

Luke, Betty. *Sadi Thread and Shisha Glass Embroidery.* Australia: Sally Milner Publishing Pty Ltd, 2001.

Mann, Kathleen. *Design from Peasant Art.* London: Adam and Charles Black, 1939.

Rivers, Victoria. *The Shining Cloth.* New York: Thames and Hudson, 1999.

Wark, Edna. *Metal Thread Embroidery.* Australia: Kangaroo Press, 1989.

North America

Paterek, Josephine. *Encyclopedia of American Indian Costume.* New York: W.W. Norton and Company, Inc, 1994.

State Historical Society of North Dakota. *Chippewa Beadwork.* Bismarck, ND: State Historical Society of North Dakota, 1996.

Mexico and Central America

Sayer, Chloe. *Arts and Crafts of Mexico.* London: Thames and Hudson, 1990.

———. *Mexican Textile Techniques.* Great Britain: Shire Publications, 1988.

Europe

Onassis, Jacqueline, editor. *In the Russian Style.* New York: MJF Books, 1976.

Sibbett, Jr., Ed. *Folk Designs for Artists and Craftspeople.* New York: Dover Publications, 1977.

Szalavary, Anne. *Hungarian Folk Designs.* New York: Dover Publications, 1980.

Turska, Jadwiga. *Polish Folk Embroidery.* Warsaw: REA, 1997.

Ugland, Thorbjorg Hjelmen. *A Sampler of Norway's Folk Costumes.* Oslo: Boksenteret A/S, 1996.

Africa

Picton, John. *The Art of African Textiles.* London: Barbicon Art Gallery with Lund Humphries Publishers, 1995.

Spring, Christopher. *African Textiles.* Rhode Island: Moyer Bell, 1997.

Ottoman Empire

Krody, Sumru Belger. *Flowers of Silk and Gold.* London: Merrell Publishers Limited, 2000.

Ross, Heather Colyer. *The Art of Arabian Costume.* Switzerland: Arabesque Commercial SA, 1994.

India

Askari, Nasreen, and Liz Arthur. *Uncut Cloth.* London: Merrell Holberton, 1999.

Grill, Rosemary. *Indian Embroidery.* London: V & A Publications, 1999.

Lynton, Linda. *The Sari.* New York: Harry N. Abrams, Inc., 1995.

Morrell, Anne. *The Techniques of Indian Embroidery.* Colorado: Interweave Press, 1995.

Far East

Chen, Lydia. *Chinese Knotting.* Republic of China: Echo Publishing Company, Ltd., 1981.

Garrett, Valery M. *Chinese Clothing.* New York: Oxford University Press, 1994.

———. *Traditional Chinese Clothing.* New York: Oxford University Press, 1987.

Keeber, Beatrice Fulton. *A Kogin Christmas.* New Jersey: DMC Corporation, 1983.

Resource List

Accomplishments
105 Louisiana Avenue
Perrysburg, OH 43551
(419) 872-9819
www.accomplishments-shop.com
Metal threads

Artemis Imports
P.O. Box 68
Pacific Grove, CA 93950
(831) 373-6762
www.artemisimports.com
Mirrors for Shisha embroidery

Carol Harris Company
1265 South Main
Dyersburg, TN 38024
(877) 269-9419
www.carolharrisco.com
Laces, linen fabric

Colonial Crafts
P.O. Box 345
Sturbridge, MA 01566
(800) 966-5524
www.colonialcrafts.com
Wool felt

Earth Guild
33 Haywood Street
Asheville, NC 28801
(800) 327-8448
www.earthguild.com
Folkwear® patterns

Farmhouse Fabrics
270 Church Road
Beech Island, SC 29842
(888) 827-1801
www.farmhousefabrics.com
Laces, linen fabric

Fire Mountain Gems
#1 Fire Mountain Way
Grants Pass, OR 97526
(800) 423-2319
www.firemountaingems.com
Beads and beading supplies

Hedgehog Handworks
P.O. Box 45384
Westchester, CA 90045
(888) 670-6040
www.hedgehoghandworks.com
Mirrors for Shisha Embroidery, pewter
closures from Norway, metal threads
(pearl purl and check purl) and pail-
lettes

Ingebretsen's Scandinavian Center
1601 East Lake Street
Minneapolis, MN 55407
(800) 279-9333
www.ingebretsens.com
Pewter closures from Norway,
Scandinavian braids and trims

Independence Needlepoint Company
470 Schooley's Mountain Road
Suite #8
Hackettstown, NJ 07840
(908) 813-0425
www.independenceneedlepoint.com
Wool tapestry yarns

Martha Pullen Company
149 Old Big Cove Road
Brownsboro, AL 35741
(800) 547-4176, ext. 2
www.marthapullen.com
Laces, linen fabric

Needlework Unlimited
3006 W. 50th Street
Minneapolis, MN 55410
(888) 925-2454
www.needleworkunlimited.bigstep.com
Wool tapestry yarns

Odden's Norsk Husflid
P.O. Box 87
Barronett, WI 54813
(800) 626-4360
www.chibardun.net/~norskhus/
Pewter closures from Norway,
Scandinavian braids and trims

Paw Prints Pattern Company
Purrfection Artistic Wearables
12323 99th Ave. N.E.
Arlington, WA 98223
(360) 653-0901
www.purrfection.com

Superior Beads
George Lokken
4521 East Superior Street
Duluth, MN 55804
(866) 267-1192
www.superiorbeads.com
Beads and beading supplies

Treadleart
25834 Narbonne Avenue
Lomita, CA 90717
(888) 322-4745
www.treadleart.com
Mirrors for Shisha embroidery

About the Author

Joan Hinds has written eight books of sewing pattern for 18" dolls. These books include a variety of costumes that range from playwear to ball gowns. The first seven books were co-authored with her former partner, Jean Becker. In 1989 they formed Fancywork and Fashion, a company that markets doll costuming books and accessories. Since Jean left the company, Joan has continued to write books and publish the company's newsletter, which features patterns and technique tips for the popular vinyl 18" doll.

Her current book, *World of Embellishment*, is a new and exciting area of study and expression. Joan has always been fascinated with folk art and cultural history. Her collection of dolls from around the world, which exhibit clothing and embellishment of other cultures, has served as the inspiration for the book.

Joan lives in Duluth, Minn. with her husband Fletcher. They have two children, Kevin and Rebecca, who are both full-time college students. For the past twelve years, Joan has been able to share her love of needlework and sewing with others by teaching classes and seminars for guilds and shops around the country. She recently served as a guest costume designer for the Duluth Playhouse.

If you would like to contact Joan —
Joan Hinds, P.O. Box 3554, Duluth, MN 55803 or www.fancyworkandfashion.com